My Journey with Justin

SHEILA K CAMPBELL

My Journey with Justin

Copyright © 2013 by Sheila K. Campbell. All rights reserved.

Editing, cover design, page formatting, and e-book by ChristianEditingServices.com.

Printed in the United States of America.

ISBN 978-0-9914767-0-1

Visit Sheila at www.PausingToPraise.com

This book is dedicated to the memory of my son Justin, whose life forever changed mine.

Table of Contents

1. A Path to Reveal the Heart   7

2. Clinging to Idols   13

3. A Bend in the Road   23

4. Surgery   29

5. A Day Etched in Memory   35

6. Unanswered Questions   41

7. Trials He Chooses   49

8. Defeated Hope   55

9. Abrupt Reality   61

10. Long Lonely Days and Nights   67

11. Home at Last   77

12. Unprepared Hearts   85

13. Unseen Scars   91

14. Losing Hope   101

15. Evidence of Providence   109

16. New Friends   117

17. Comfort in an Ancient Story   123

18. Abandoned Again   131

19. Breaking Ground   141

20. Unexpected Relief   147

21. Uncontrolled Anger   153

22. Desires that Heal   159

23. The Beginning of Balance   167

24. Looking for Answers   179

25. A Handicapped Heart   185

26. Growing Gratitude for Roads Not Traveled   195

27. A Renewed Search for Answers   205

28. Lessons in Unconditional Love   213

29. Joyful Labor   219

30. Desperate Situations and
    Miserable Mistakes   227

31. Happy Pills   233

32. Abundant Blessings   239

33. New Help   251

34. Peace and Beauty   257

35. Dark Days   265

36. Adjusting to Change   275

37. Life Lessons Continue   285

38. Difficult Decisions   293

39. Farewell   301

40. Remembering   311

☞ Chapter 1 ☜

A Path to Reveal the Heart

People may be pure in their own eyes,
but the Lord examines their motives.
Proverbs 16:2

"Watch me!" The words rang out through the bright spring sunshine as my redheaded fireball of energy sped past on his bike. Justin had learned to ride the bike late in the summer right before his fifth birthday, but winter's cold had forced the boy and the bike to wait until warmer days to resume their journeys on the dusty farm roads surrounding the old house where we lived.

However, spring had arrived at last. I stood just inside the door and watched in wonder as his hands tightly gripped the handlebars and his legs peddled furiously down the dirt driveway. It was April 1992. Less than a week earlier, Justin had coded on the table during a cardiac catheterization; his heart had stopped as the small tube attempted to pass through the non-existent pulmonary valve. The physicians had immediately withdrawn the catheter and worked to revive his small body. He had spent the night in the ICU, where his energy and his comical outgoing personality soon had the nurses on the night shift enamored. His curiosity was difficult to squelch in a room full of buttons. Not long after arriving on the floor, he had managed to push a code alert button, which brought a crash cart and nurses running from all directions. His punishment from the doting nurses was ice cream and a movie.

The catheterization required a small incision in the groin area; however, because of scar tissue from previous catheterizations, the doctors were unable to insert the tube and had to repeat the procedure in another vein on the opposite side. As a result, Justin had come home with a couple of stitches in the groin on each leg. Yet his high tolerance for pain and his zeal for life had him speeding past on his bike just days later as though nothing had happened—stitches still in place. I knew I should stop him and force him to entertain himself calmly, but I was mesmerized by his high energy. So as he laughed in the bright sunshine, I stood watching him and tried to memorize the moment.

Justin would soon face another open-heart surgery to replace the defective pulmonary valve. In fact, we had been sent home to wait until the hospital could locate a suitable transplant as it was determined that a human transplant would be the best choice for Justin. Although we were no strangers to hospitals, I could not completely dispel the icy fingers of fear that clutched at my heart. From somewhere deep within I felt a growing dread.

"Robby," I whispered one night after we had gone to bed. "I have a bad feeling about this surgery. I've never been this afraid for one of our boys before. I dreaded Justin's first surgery, but something's different this time. I just feel real uneasy about this surgery." I stared into the dark and waited for his reply, hoping he would help alleviate my fear.

"If it will make you feel any better, I've felt the same way every time one of our boys has been in the hospital. I never feel good about it until they are home," Robby said quietly, trying to dispel my fears. "It will be over soon and hopefully Justin won't have to have any more surgeries." His words were unusually tender, but they did not still my quaking heart.

Just weeks earlier, I had taken both Justin and Jacob to our local doctor with symptoms of allergies and asthma. Dr. Linton had been our family doctor for many years and she was both compassionate and professional. While examining the boys, she asked, "When was the last time they saw their cardiologist?"

"A little over two years," I confessed. "I wish I could find another pediatric cardiologist. The one we see doesn't tell me much. He seems irritated with my questions and he's difficult to understand, so I don't want to repeat myself and I leave with my questions unanswered." I reluctantly admitted, "We had to cancel the last appointment because of a conflict and I just never rescheduled."

"You always have the right to change doctors; I do think they need to see a cardiologist," she said patiently. "I think what we're seeing today is simply allergy related asthma, but I would feel better if they kept regular appointments with a pediatric cardiologist. There's a new one in Lubbock. I don't know much about her, but I would be happy to make an appointment for your boys." Before I left that day, the boys had an appointment.

I dreaded the first appointment. Initially, I was concerned more about Jacob and the doctor's recommendation for him than I was about Justin. Justin seemed to be strong and healthy, while Jacob was still small for his age and often sickly. Before the appointment, I spent much time in prayer—especially for Jacob. We were surprised when their test results came back and the cardiologist said she was unable to locate any evidence of Jacob's atrial septal defect (ASD)—effectively a hole in his heart that was discovered on an echocardiogram soon after his birth. We were told that although it is rare, occasionally an ASD closes as a baby grows. Our new cardiologist determined he had some pulmonary insufficiency, but overall, he seemed fine. Allergies and asthma were a far greater concern for him than his minor heart condition. Justin on the other hand still had severe pulmonary stenosis. The valve they had opened as a newborn was now nothing more than a small slit, and his heart that was enlarged at birth was still considerably enlarged and appeared to be under tremendous stress.

I was taken aback at the news. Justin appeared to be energetic and healthy. He always had good color to his face and lips and just didn't have the appearance of a child who suffered from a severe heart condition. But Jacob was calm and rarely chose energetic play. He struggled with allergies, and it was always difficult to tell if the bluish color under his eyes was a symptom of a heart condition or asthma.

Despite my surprise and the growing dread deep within my heart, I convinced myself that if we must face another trial in our lives, God had chosen my strongest and healthiest child. So I stood there watching Justin playing that day, the moment forever etched in my mind. I watched his red hair glisten in the bright sun and smiled at the freckles splattered across his checks. I thanked the Lord for his red hair, his dancing blue eyes, his seemingly endless energy, his love for Legos, and his curious nature that made him approach the world so carefully observant, asking endless questions and making funny comments. I was thankful for everything about him. In my prayer that day, I told God that should he choose to take Justin from me, I was thankful for the years I had been given to love and raise him. The gratitude was genuine; however, it was a prayer of feigned piety—I truly believed if I freely offered Justin to God and if God saw I was willing to let go of him, then surely he would allow me to hold on to my precious son.

My prayer was an attempt to earn God's mercy. My greatest desire was that he would spare my son and alleviate my fears. I just could not imagine that a loving God would take my child and not allow him to grow up. I never imagined any other consequence of surgery—it was a matter of life or death and nothing else even entered my thoughts. I told myself that God knew I had vowed to raise all my children in the fear and admonition of the Lord—but just to be certain, I reminded him daily in my prayers, confident that my vow could win favor.

Looking back, I know the Lord heard those prayers. He knew my heart and where my hope lay far better than I. It was a loving and merciful God who set me on a journey that would slowly open my eyes to the condition of my own heart.

Chapter 2

Clinging to Idols

A third time he asked him, "Simon son of John, do you love me?"
Peter was hurt that Jesus asked the question a third time.
He said, "Lord, you know everything. You know that I love you."
Jesus said, "Then feed my sheep."
John 21:17

Justin was born August 7, 1986. With his birth, I began a journey that would take me through countless valleys and over many jagged mountains. This journey with God was not the only journey I would take—there would be others—but this would prove to be one of the longest and most difficult.

Justin had his first open-heart surgery when he was only a few weeks old. Had he been born in a larger hospital, he would have had surgery when he was only a few days old. Perhaps due partly to ignorance and youth, and largely to God's grace and mercy, I had an incredible peace when he went in for that first surgery. I had crumbled with fear and anxiety when we were told he had to have heart surgery, but the fear quickly dissipated. A week later I sat quietly in the waiting room visiting with family while surgeons labored for hours on my infant son. Justin recovered quickly and was soon a happy, healthy baby. We continued to follow up with his cardiology appointments, but life had once more settled into a comfortable routine that required neither great measures of faith nor blinders to reality.

Just four days after Justin's second birthday, Jacob was born—four weeks premature. He had underdeveloped lungs and a poorly developed digestive system. He also suffered from severe jaundice. When Jacob was two weeks old, he too was diagnosed with a congenital heart defect. Justin had severe pulmonary stenosis and a small atrium sepal defect, but Jacob had a larger atrium sepal defect and some pulmonary insufficiency. Their problems were different but obviously hereditary. Although Jacob's defect wasn't as severe as Justin's and he didn't require immediate surgery, I struggled with the diagnosis. The reality that there were circumstances in life beyond my control filled me with fear and anxiety I could not bring myself to face. So I treated Jacob like a normal baby and tried to ignore his problems, but at seven months, he weighed only ten pounds and was labeled with failure to thrive. Because of his poor health, surgery to close the hole between the upper two chambers of his heart was delayed. He seemed sickly and weak. Deep within my heart I had a fear of losing Jacob—a fear I could not allow myself to face.

On the other hand, Justin seemed to be strong and healthy despite his severe heart condition. He was rarely sick, and if it were not for the scar running the length of his chest, he would appear to be a normal, energetic little boy. We knew exactly what was wrong with Justin though he displayed no obvious symptoms. Jacob was different. I could not put my faith in doctors to heal him or make him better because they simply didn't know what was wrong or why he was not gaining weight. So it was through Jacob that God began to stretch my faith. It was a tiny grain of faith mixed with unacknowledged fear and avoidance, but those difficult circumstances planted a tiny seed in my heart that desired real faith. I knew I feared my own decisions and I longed to have a genuine trust in the Lord to direct those choices.

It was years later before we would discover that the majority of Jacob's problems were allergy and digestive related. It would also take years before I could trust that the Lord was sovereign over my decisions regardless of my inexperience, immaturity, and selfish motives.

When Jacob was just fifteen months old and Justin barely three, Jerrod was born to our growing family. Like Jacob, Jerrod arrived prematurely. He was airlifted from our small rural hospital to a larger hospital nearby when his lungs collapsed shortly after birth. Unlike Jacob, Jerrod's recovery was quick and complete.

Taking care of three boys was a full-time job—one I enjoyed thoroughly. I felt my life was complete, and I was extremely thankful for each of my boys. They were the live baby dolls I had always dreamed of, and I was continually awestruck at the gift of life bundled in the package of a little boy. It was during these days of babies and toddlers and living a life that seemed to fulfill my heart's deepest desires that I inadvertently discovered that a grateful heart was a deeply joyful heart. I loved my babies. In fact, they were the love of my life. I could not imagine life without them—and so I didn't. I often avoided doctor check-ups and any situation that reminded me life could be fragile. But God was gracious: Jacob began to improve, and the boys were happy and healthy most of the time.

I enjoyed caring for my boys and was sometimes surprised when others assumed I would enjoy some time away from them. My mother-in-law, "Mamma" to my children, often generously offered to keep the boys so I could make a weekly trip to town to buy groceries and run errands. When I accepted her offer, I did appreciate the help, but I also missed them even when I was gone for only a few hours. Consequently, I did not always mention when I was planning a trip to town. (Looking back, I never considered that others might also enjoy their company.)

One bright spring morning, I painstakingly dressed the boys in white shirts for a trip to town. Justin and Jacob wore navy shorts I had made from a scrap of material my mother had given me, and Jerrod was decked out in a navy one-piece jumper I had made from some inexpensive cotton. I felt as though I was playing house with my very own little babies, dressing them up and toting them to town to show them off.

That particular morning we left early and arrived at Walmart just as their studio opened. I carried Jerrod in his carrier and Jacob on my hip. Justin dutifully clung to the handle of the carrier until I could reach a shopping cart and deposit them all inside. I think the young girl at the photography studio was a bit overwhelmed at the idea of photographing a group picture of three small boys, ages five months, twenty months, and three years. But I chattered while she arranged them in various settings, and the boys smiled and laughed and we all enjoyed the whole process. Jerrod, who was a particularly happy baby, smiled at everything. Although Jacob was timid, he was put at ease by his older brother, who jabbered nonstop. Justin would try in his best big brotherly voice to assure Jacob, and then he'd turn to the photographer and tell her everything his three-year-old mind could conceive to say about his younger brothers. She soon knew their first, middle, and last names as well as their favorite foods and sleeping habits. And, of course, she knew his daddy drove a tractor and was pre-watering fields for planting. She was quite enamored with the boys, and we were blessed with an assortment of adorable pictures to commemorate the occasion.

The boys were my constant companions, and my life was completely devoted to their routines. I took immense pleasure in serving them and caring for them, but life was more than just meeting their needs—I loved just spending time with them. We read nursery rhymes, went on nature walks, and enjoyed snack time together. Whatever I did— whether it was doing laundry or dishes or working in the yard—they were right there with me. Although our budget was very limited, I loved shopping for them and would often do without so I could occasionally purchase matching outfits or a special toy. Among the favorites were three Tonka dump trucks. Justin's imagination often converted them into fire trucks or monster trucks or anything else that would make noise as the three of them pushed the dump trucks about the house or yard as fast as they could go, Jacob and Jerrod loudly imitating Justin's siren or roaring engine.

Of course, raising three small boys was not without its trials and challenges. I was strict and sometimes impatient with them. I was so eager to see them grow and develop that many times my expectations were beyond their abilities and their years. Despite my shortcomings, the Lord continued to be gracious to our little family, and we enjoyed much happiness—but often had to come up with creative ways to manage them.

Once such time occurred when Jerrod was just a toddler and Justin not quite five. We took our little family on a camping trip to the mountains. It was the height of the summer and we had not reserved a camping spot, so the only available place was situated between the river and the highway. This meant we would have to keep an eye on the boys at all times—particularly our two curious and energetic ones—to keep them a safe distance from both the highway and the river. Jacob was not yet three, but he had always been able to engage in quiet play with only a few simple toys for long stretches of time. However, both Justin and Jerrod were busy and inquisitive and never stayed in one spot for more than a few seconds. On that particular occasion, we had brought some small tractors and trucks. Robby and I quickly unloaded their toys, hoping they could entertain themselves playing in the dirt while we set up the campsite.

"Here, boys," I called as I pulled out a box of small tractors and trucks. "You build me a farm while Daddy and I unload the car and set up a tent for us."

But Justin and Jerrod were far too excited to occupy themselves for long with toys from home. Just minutes later I heard Justin shout, "Hey Jacob, look at this!" He was about thirty feet away holding up a large rock for his brother—who was still sitting by the box of toys—to see.

"Justin, you need to sit right here and play with these toys," I directed as he came running up with his rock. But while I was speaking, Jerrod was toddling away to look at pinecones.

I made a few more futile attempts to interest the boys in the toys I had brought, but there were too many sticks, pinecones, rocks, and other treasures competing for their attention. We were far too busy trying to corral the boys to finish the unloading and get our camp set up. Finally, in an act of desperation, we tied a piece of rope around Justin's and Jerrod's waists and tied them to a nearby tree so we could get the tent set up without losing sight of them. Although I have no memories of any further difficulties on that trip, I have often recalled that particular creative solution.

I remember those days as bright and joyous. Of course, there were also difficult days, financial struggles, and numerous trials mingled in, but I have countless memories of simple moments that I treasured: backyard picnics, sandboxes, and frogs. Sitting on the tailgate of the pickup while my husband set aluminum irrigation tubes for the cotton and corn. Little boys running barefoot in the dusty road backlit by the setting sun. Enjoying moonlit evenings on the porch explaining the wonders of the night sky to wide-eyed little boys.

My children satisfied my desire for meaning and purpose, and that satisfaction brought me great pleasure.

While I viewed them as a precious gift from God, I was often tempted to love and cling to the gift more than the giver.

I remember the first time as a parent I was exposed to the tragedy of parents losing their child. A doctor in our community and his wife lost their teenage son in a tragic auto accident. My faith was left raw and bare . . . and I glimpsed the weakness of my own heart. I could not understand why a loving God would allow such horrific heartache to strike a good Christian family. I wondered if perhaps it was a result of poor decisions—maybe he shouldn't have left the house that day—or perhaps it was some kind of judgment or punishment for secret sins. I also considered that perhaps they weren't grateful for what they had and so God took it away from them.

I never completely acknowledged my judgments nor was I able to come to any confident conclusions, but unanswered questions left my faith floundering. If there were no reasonable answers, then it could only mean that we served a God who was not sovereign, who didn't care, or who might allow—and even purpose—difficult circumstances for his children . . . none of which I wanted to believe.

While their loss gave me an even deeper sense of value for my own children and I clung to them even more tightly than I had before, it also sent me looking for answers to squelch my doubts and fears about God. I desperately wanted to believe that I served a God who truly cared and controlled the circumstances of my life and would protect us from tragedy and pain—or at least that is what I thought I wanted. Later I would realize what I had really wanted was a God who had only good things for me, things that *I* viewed to be good like healthy, obedient, happy children.

In the years that lay ahead, I would learn that God is sovereign despite our weaknesses . . . that good things—things that draw our hearts to him—may not always look good on the outside and may appear difficult . . . and that he cares so much he uses every circumstance in our lives to show us his love and his glory. God would slowly and gently show me that all the things we claim as our own belong to us only because they have been freely given to us. They are given in the perfect condition for our hearts to best receive them. While they may appear to be imperfect, they are exactly what we need. Furthermore, they are gifts—not something we deserve or don't deserve—but perfect gifts from a loving father. We need only to stop and recognize them as such. This recognition of our abundant gifts despite our own unworthiness is where true gratitude begins—a gratitude that lifts our eyes off the gift and turns our hearts to the giver. In the years that lay ahead, many times the words of Job would pass through my thoughts: "The Lord gave, and the Lord hath taken away; blessed be the name of the Lord" (Job 1:21). Later, when the entire world was black and those bright rays of the sun seemed to be forever shrouded, the Lord would bring to my mind the gratitude and praise I once offered for those days of sunshine, and I would have to ask myself if I could still say, "Blessed be the name of the Lord."

I wish I could honestly say I have learned to love the giver more than the gifts, but I continue to struggle with that even today. Just when I think I can say, "Nothing but you Lord, nothing but you," I find my heart clinging once more to my children. As the years pass, I often find myself wondering what the honest answer of my heart would be were the Lord to ask me as he asked Peter, "Lovest thou me more than these?"

I am so thankful he continues to pursue my heart. As I lift my eyes to behold his glory, I discover that which I hold so tightly is only dust. Those things that last, he holds for me.

⋟ Chapter 3 ⋞

A Bend in the Road

We can make our plans, but the Lord determines our steps.
Proverbs 16:9

In August of 1991, Justin turned five and was ready to start school. Unwilling to part with his company for several hours a day, I suggested we homeschool him, and Robby consented. I loved teaching Justin new things and he enjoyed learning. After using a variety of workbooks and supplemental materials in the fall, we ordered a complete kindergarten curriculum with our Christmas bonus that winter. Justin whizzed through the kindergarten workbooks and was quickly learning to read. He had been memorizing poems and scripture since he was three, so he was quick to memorize sight words. He loved music and knew the words to every song on the children's cassettes we owned and several popular country songs he heard on the radio. He could also tie his shoes, and we took the training wheels off his bike a month before his fifth birthday.

Like all parents, I was proud of Justin's five-year-old accomplishments. It was fun watching him grow out of those preschool years. As spring approached, we were looking forward to completing kindergarten, the glorious days of summer, and the arrival of a new baby. Although we did not know the sex of the child I was carrying, Justin was certain it would be a little sister.

When we learned we could no longer put off another surgery, I wanted to hold on to the bright spring days and not think about what lay ahead. I tried to tell myself it would all be over quickly and in two weeks Justin would be back home. In six weeks he would be completely recovered and we could start preparing for the birth of our fourth child and all the bright days beyond. But the surgery loomed ahead like an ominous cloud.

Because the doctors were trying to locate a human heart valve, we had returned home after Justin's cardiac catheterization to wait. Two weeks later we received a call. "Mrs. Campbell?" the voice of a young lady asked sweetly.

"Yes."

"The doctor has located a heart valve for your son, and he would like you to bring Justin in tomorrow for his pre-op tests and blood work." Her words filled me with dread and fear.

"Tomorrow?"

"Yes, they're having it shipped here today." In a daze, I agreed to an appointment time and hung up the phone slowly, trying to steel myself for what lay ahead.

That evening my mother-in-law came and picked up Jacob and Jerrod. After finishing up laundry and carefully packing Justin's clothes and a few toys, he and I stepped out into the cool spring evening and planted tomatoes in the garden without the "assistance" of his younger brothers. While I walked along the rows digging holes for the young plants, Justin followed behind me setting the plants into the holes, painstakingly covering the roots with dirt and patting the moist earth firm with his small hands. When we were done, Justin looked on his work with satisfaction and began talking about eating fresh tomatoes straight from the garden.

On May 5, 1992, Justin, my mother, and I arrived at the hospital. We parked in the parking garage and, much to Justin's delight, walked across the sky bridge to the hospital. To his Nana's amazement, Justin led us down the maze of hospital corridors to the reception room where we had filled out paperwork and started his battery of tests prior to his cardiac catheterization two weeks earlier. His cardiologist met us there to give us directions to where we needed to check him into the hospital and explain the few tests that would need to be repeated before his surgery.

Understandably, Justin disliked all the pre-op tests and blood work, but he had a high tolerance for pain and an inquisitive nature that made the whole process seem like an adventure. When a young phlebotomist stuck his arm and began to fill a syringe with blood, Justin stared wide-eyed as the syringe filled and asked, "Are you going to pull out all my blood?" Having a rare blood type like his father, Justin had watched his daddy and his Aunt Cammy give blood earlier that would be used for his surgery. He seemed to think that he might be short on blood. As he watched the phlebotomist, Justin was a bit concerned that the young gentleman might be inclined to take more than he was willing to part with.

Although having his blood drawn was a bit scary, Justin's biggest fear was that the wire from his first surgery, which could be felt just beneath the skin on his chest, would get "messed up." He loved to show people how a small bit of wire not covered by bone would allow a refrigerator magnet to stick to his chest. He repeatedly asked his cardiologist and anyone else who would listen if they could make sure they left his wire in place.

Once we were settled into a room, Justin enjoyed the attention he was receiving. He was building what he called a "masher truck" with Legos and chatted with everyone who entered the room about his creation and how it would work. Daddy, Mamma, Grandpa, and his brothers all came to visit. All three boys sat on the bed and played with cars and Justin's newest Lego creation. With lots of company and attention, Justin didn't even seem to notice that he had missed supper. Later that evening after everyone had gone, Justin stood on the window bench and gazed out in wonder at the city lights. To the small country boy who had only known the night sky to be lit with moonlight and stars, the brilliance of the city lights was mesmerizing from his lofty view.

It had been a long day and the stress of the situation, combined with my pregnancy, had left me completely exhausted, but the small cot in Justin's room did not look inviting. I had managed to slip out the room and eat supper while family entertained Justin. I would have fasted with Justin, but I knew that without something to eat, the morning sickness I had fought for months would return. Robby had gone to his sister's apartment nearby to sleep and would return in the wee hours of the morning before Justin was prepped for surgery. As night fell, Justin drifted off to sleep after his usual bedtime story with a loose grip on his favorite companion—a stuffed monkey named Micky. I suddenly felt very alone. I prayed for the strength to endure, but my prayers seemed to stop at the ceiling and echo silently back into the darkness.

The next morning before the gray light of dawn had pierced the blackness of night, Robby arrived in Justin's room just ahead of the doctor. A nurse arrived to start Justin's IV, and the anesthesiologist came in to let Justin pick out the "flavor" of his gas mask and to brief us on the procedures. Both the surgeon and the doctor reviewed the surgery with us once more. There were a few more papers to sign acknowledging that we were aware of the risks involved in the procedure. Yes, we were aware of the risks but felt helpless to make any other choice.

Soon we were all headed down the hall on our way to surgery—a moment that would be remembered by all involved. On the way to surgery, Justin talked about his stuffed monkey and the new baby he hoped would be a little sister. "I think we should name her Jessica so I can call her Jesse. I know a Jesse on TV," he said matter-of-factly.

I smiled at his statement and reminded him, "But I want to name a little girl Jennifer. Don't you think Mama should get to pick her name if we have a baby girl?"

He looked up at me from the gurney and thought about it for a moment before he replied. "Okay, you can use Jennifer, but I'm still going to call her Jesse."

Robby laughed. "Looks like you might lose out on that one," he said, looking at me, then grinning back at Justin.

We waited beside the gurney until the doctors were ready. Then as they wheeled him through the doors into surgery, Robby and I both kissed his head. "I love you," I said softly.

"We'll be right here when you wake up," Robby assured him.

Already groggy from the anesthetics, he murmured, "I love you too."

They were the last words we would ever hear him speak.

≈ Chapter 4 ≈

Surgery

Even when I walk through the darkest valley,
I will not be afraid, for you are close beside me.
Your rod and your staff protect and comfort me.
Psalms 23:4

Shortly after parting with Justin, Robby and I made our way to the waiting room to begin our vigil. To our surprise, we found the waiting room full of friends and family, all waiting for news. We tried to answer questions as best we could and went over what Justin's doctor and surgeon had told us about the surgery. It was a very difficult and complex surgery and would take eight to nine hours to complete. Our family and friends gathered and Rev. Bruce Keller, a dear pastor and friend, led us all in prayer, asking for guidance for the surgeon and strength for Justin. As he prayed for a quick and complete recovery, I silently agreed with him. I could not let myself think of any other outcome.

Almost two hours later, we had our first report from the

operating room. It had taken longer than anticipated to open Justin's chest cavity because of a large amount of scar tissue from his previous surgery as an infant. This would delay the procedure.

The day wore away slowly. Every few hours we would be updated on the progress of the operation. Someone went to get sandwiches for lunch. Occasionally another friend or family member would arrive to see how things were going. Family members took turns entertaining Jacob and Jerrod, and for once, I didn't fret about whom they were with or where they were going. I knew they were being looked after and that was all that mattered. I talked quietly with family and friends but later could not remember any of the conversations. Meanwhile, the clock ticked away the hours.

Finally, late in the afternoon, the report came: the operation was over and they were closing his chest. We were told the surgeon would soon come to give us a report. When at last the surgeon stepped out and told us they were moving Justin to the ICU, I breathed a quiet sigh. I felt as though I had been holding my breath for hours, but I knew from experience that Justin would still be critical for several hours. The surgeon let us know the new valve seemed to be working correctly and Justin was stable. They had roused him just enough to get him to respond to a few simple commands and then sedated him again to keep him comfortable. It all looked good and we would be able to see him soon.

Less than an hour later, we were led down a long hall to a back entrance of the ICU. Justin looked so very small and pale lying there in that big hospital bed. He was on a ventilator and had a chest drainage tube, a catheter, and several monitor leads coming out from his unfastened hospital gown. He also had IV lines and an O_2 monitor attached to his small arm and hand. The machines beeped a steady rhythm as I bent to kiss his forehead and run my hand over his short red hair. The scene was familiar, and I felt an odd sense of relief knowing that the surgery I had dreaded was now over. Justin was alive and stable and now we could focus on recovery.

One by one Grandpa and Mamma (Robby's parents) and Papa and Nana (my parents) came in and stood beside his bed for a few minutes. Mamma and Nana each kissed his forehead in much the same way as I had done. A few other family members were allowed a brief glimpse. Robby and I were told we could come and go as we pleased as long as we used the back entrance. We took turns getting a bite to eat, saying good-bye to the boys and family. Then we settled in Justin's room to sit with him for a while.

Justin seemed to be stable, so around midnight we slipped into the waiting room to try to get a few hours of sleep. Soon I was fast asleep despite the brightly lit room and the night sounds of the hospital, but I awoke with a start. I wasn't sure how long I had been asleep, but I noticed that Robby was gone. I headed toward Justin's room and saw Robby in the hall talking to the surgeon. I knew instantly that something was wrong. Someone ushered us into a small, beautifully furnished room, and a hospital chaplain greeted us.

The surgeon told us Justin had taken a turn for the worse when he received a blood transfusion that his body rejected. Justin had a rare blood type, so Robby and two of his siblings had given blood prior to Justin's surgery. However, that blood had been used during surgery. When Justin's blood pressure had dropped during the night, the decision was made to give him blood from a universal donor, but his reaction to the transfusion was severe. The hospital's chaplain sat and prayed with us as the doctors worked on Justin. A short time later, a doctor entered the room and asked Robby if he would be willing to donate blood once again for Justin even though he had already given less than two weeks earlier. Of course, there wasn't even a need to ask. Robby quickly followed the doctor and offered his own life-giving blood for his son.

By midmorning Justin was once again stable. Robby and I were both exhausted, so when family began arriving again early that morning, we let them sit with Justin while we changed clothes and freshened up in the hospital restrooms. We grabbed a bite to eat in the hospital cafeteria and brought it back up to where we were camping out in the waiting room. We tried to doze a bit, but it was difficult with the continual stream of visitors. It was such a blessing to have so many people who were concerned and cared enough to stop in and see how he was doing. Several friends gave us cash for meals, gas, and other necessities, while others brought snacks and things to make our hospital stay more bearable. Many people tried to encourage us by reminding us that the time in the ICU was the hardest part of the stay and that Justin would soon be in a room. I consoled myself by remembering Justin's first surgery required only three days in the ICU. The scare of the evening had subsided, and I began looking forward to Justin weaning off the ventilator and moving to a room. I didn't want him to suffer any pain, but I couldn't wait until he was once again conscious and talking to us.

Both sets of grandparents took turns keeping Jacob and Jerrod and visiting the hospital. Although I missed them terribly, I was glad the boys were able to stay where they were well cared for and happy. I knew that after three nights away, they both would be missing home. But if they had to stay somewhere, I was thankful it was with grandparents with whom they were comfortable.

As the day passed, Justin began to show improvement, and the doctors began the process of weaning him down off the ventilator. His setback the night before had slowed his recovery a little, but he was strong. By evening, his doctors seemed pleased with his progress. That night Robby and I were able to get a little more sleep in the waiting room despite the lights and flow of people in and out. There were family members of other ICU patients also sleeping and keeping vigil throughout the night, so it was generally quiet. We were so exhausted that any sleep felt good. Early the next morning, I washed my hair in the bathroom sink and once again changed clothes before visitors started arriving. Robby and I kept a change of clothes in a tote that he carried to the pickup once a day. The walk to the parking garage was about as far as either of us would venture during those first critical days.

⌒ Chapter 5 ⌒

A Day Etched in Memory

But even in darkness I cannot hide from you.
To you the night shines as bright as day.
Darkness and light are the same to you.
Psalm 139:12

Day two in the ICU passed uneventfully. Justin continued to wean slowly off his dependence on the ventilator and breathe more and more on his own. By evening his doctors were predicting that he would be completely off sometime the next day. We were told that once he was off the ventilator he would probably be moved to a room within a day or two. I couldn't wait—I wasn't sure how many more nights I could spend sleeping in the ICU waiting room.

Day three dawned much like the others: I awoke to a well-lit waiting room and stark white halls. There were no windows in the waiting room or anywhere within view of the ICU, so it was difficult to judge the passage of time or the time of day except for the large clock on the wall above the information desk. Although everything was white and the artificial lights lit every corner of the room and the hallways, I felt as though I was in a cave. I could not wait to get out into the bright spring sunshine.

Justin was doing well that morning, and his doctors were continuing to wean him down with hopes of taking him off the ventilator later that day. It was Saturday and Robby's sister and her husband, Dwain, had offered us the use of their apartment to shower and relax while they sat with Justin. Since Justin was doing so well and we both wanted to be there when they took him off of the ventilator, which we were told might be sometime that afternoon, we decided to take them up on their offer. It was the first time we had left the hospital since his surgery four days earlier.

It had rained on and off the week before Justin went into the hospital, and although it was May, we had worn light jackets to the hospital. The air-conditioned hospital and waiting room found me reaching often for my jacket, so I eagerly anticipated the warm sunshine and a chance to walk outside for even just a few moments. The possibility of a shower was also very inviting. And the thought that Justin might actually be conscious before the end of the day appeared like a ray of sunshine at the end of a long tunnel.

We decided to head straight to the apartment, shower, and then go eat lunch somewhere nice before heading back to the hospital. I showered first and stood a long time letting the warm water sooth my tense muscles. I rubbed my swollen belly and hoped that the stress of the hospital visit was not too hard on the child I carried. Dr. Linton had said that the timing of Justin's surgery could not have been better since I was in the middle of my second trimester. Having delivered the boys early, my pregnancy was considered high-risk, and she felt that stress of this nature in my last trimester might be difficult on the baby and me. She was anxious to see our family settle back into routine before my last trimester and was hopeful that Justin would be fully recovered before my due date.

I had just stepped out of the shower and was getting dressed when I heard Robby on the phone. He rapped on the door and said, "Hurry, we need to get back to the hospital!"

We quickly gathered up our things and headed back. Justin was doing so well when we left, I just couldn't imagine what could have gone wrong. It seemed unreal that there would be a problem at this point.

When we arrived at the hospital, Dwain and Cammy met us in the ICU waiting room. They weren't sure what was going on or what exactly had happened. Justin's cardiologist had come in to check on Justin's progress shortly after we left. She seemed to think that he was doing well enough to go ahead and remove the ventilator, but when the tube was pulled, Justin didn't seem to respond well. That was when Dwain and Cammy were asked to leave.

Robby and I didn't wait for an invitation—we headed straight for Justin's room. When we entered the unit, we could hear a commotion and saw several doctors and nurses gathered around Justin's bed. They seemed to all be talking at once although I couldn't understand what they were saying. I caught sight of the nurse in charge of Justin's care and she was visibly upset. The charge nurse over the unit was also at his bed and her cheeks were flushed red. When she turned and saw us, she quickly ushered us out of the unit and told us she would let the doctor know we were there. Robby tried to protest, but she motioned to another nurse to help usher us to the waiting room.

Within minutes, Justin's cardiologist and a doctor we had never seen came to talk to us. The explanation was very brief. We were told that his cardiologist had tried to take Justin off of the ventilator, but when the tube was removed, he was not conscious enough to breathe on his own. An attempt to rouse him had been made, but it was unsuccessful and so the ventilator had been replaced and was once again at full capacity. It also appeared that Justin might have some fluid in his lungs, so chest x-rays had been ordered. Once the x-rays were done, we would be able to go sit with him again.

We used the phone in the waiting room to call family. We told them the doctors had tried to take Justin off of the ventilator but apparently he wasn't quite ready. We explained they had to replace the tube and it was once again back on full capacity, so it could be several more days before they would be able to wean him back down again and actually get him off the ventilator.

When the chest x-rays were complete, we were finally allowed back into his room. A pulmonologist explained to us that Justin had pneumonia and a chest drainage tube had been inserted to help drain some of the fluid from his lungs. When I asked if his lung had collapsed, he looked surprised at the question and told me I would need to discuss the details of Justin's condition with his doctor. I had asked because Jerrod had a chest drainage tube when his lungs had collapsed soon after birth. I never got a definite answer.

A few of the other families in the ICU waiting room approached us throughout the day with questions about what had happened. Apparently, several had noticed the commotion and were concerned. We simply relayed the information we had been told. One lady, whose young adult son was in the unit, asked, "Is Justin okay? Did he code?"

"No one said anything to us about that. We don't really know what happened, but I'm certain if Justin had coded, someone would have told us." I assured her.

"Well, I was sitting with my son when they asked your family to leave. Then a little while later they asked us to leave and they were bringing the crash cart to Justin's unit." She continued, "We're praying he'll be okay. He's such a cute little boy."

I would remember her question later and the missing answer would haunt me.

The rest of the day was quiet. Justin's nurses had been very friendly and would often spend time talking to us while they monitored Justin and recorded his stats, but that day everyone was unusually quiet. When it was time for the nurses to change shifts, we were asked to leave. After the first night, we had been allowed to stay during shift change as long as we stayed out of the way, so it seemed an unusual request. While we were out of the room, I thought I caught a glimpse of Justin's surgeon leaving the ICU unit and striding hurriedly down the hall, but we never again saw or spoke to his surgeon during his hospital stay.

By evening, Justin appeared to be stable—the machines once more breathing steadily for him—and Robby and I spent another night in the ICU waiting room.

☞ Chapter 6 ☜

Unanswered Questions

_____

"Destruction and Death say, 'We've heard only rumors of where wisdom can be found.' God alone understands the way to wisdom; he knows where it can be found."
Job 28:22-23

The morning following the failed attempt at extubation was Mother's Day. The night had passed uneventfully with Justin's ventilator set at full capacity. Jacob and Jerrod had been staying with grandparents for a week now and I missed them terribly. My parents currently had them and planned to bring them to the hospital for a visit. I couldn't wait to see them!

I awoke wondering when the doctors would determine to start the process of weaning Justin off the ventilator once again. The setback of the day before was so bitterly disappointing. I was getting very homesick and couldn't wait until Justin was on the mend and we could all go home. I longed to just be home with my boys. I wanted to sit out on the porch and watch them play in the warm spring sunshine.

I wanted to work in the garden and enjoy the simple pleasures of life. Justin had been in the hospital six days and already it seemed like an eternity. Robby reminded me that the doctor had originally said to plan on staying ten days to two weeks and with the setbacks he had undergone, we should be prepared to stay even a bit longer. So I tried to focus my thoughts on Justin's recovery and not be anxious about going home.

That morning I once again washed my hair in the bathroom sink and did my best to freshen up without a shower. A hospital orderly had offered Robby access to the employee showers on another floor the night before since he hadn't been able to shower before we were called back to the hospital. I had stayed with Justin so I did not know where the showers were nor did I feel comfortable using them.

Even if the accommodations were not ideal, it was nice to freshen up and change clothes. I was anxious to see Justin's doctor, so I wanted to get to his bedside early. His cardiologist was usually the one who would take a few minutes to talk to us when she did her rounds and update us on his progress and prognosis. Occasionally, an intern or other doctor assigned to some aspect of his care would discuss his care with us, but that was generally left up to his primary physician, who was his cardiologist. We had not seen her since her brief explanation about the problems extubating him the day before, and I wanted to know her prognosis.

I took the back way and arrived at Justin's bedside before morning shift change. The nurse in charge of Justin's care had gently folded back the blanket covering Justin's feet and legs and was massaging his feet. Justin's feet seemed oddly stiff. As I approached, the nurse looked up from her work and there were tears in her eyes. I was a taken aback and asked her what was wrong.

"He's posturing," she said with controlled emotion. I felt suddenly numb—as though I were walking in a fog—but I had to know. "I don't understand what that means. Can you please tell me what that means?"

"I shouldn't be the one to tell you this," she said quietly. "I thought they would talk to you about it yesterday . . ." She paused. "It's a sign of brain damage. You really need to talk to his doctor. We'll make sure she knows you want to talk to her." Then she fell silent.

I looked at Justin's feet again and tried to process what she had said. I'm not sure how long I stood there before Robby came in. The nurse was now charting at the foot of Justin's bed, and I repeated to him what she had told me. Without missing a beat, Robby began peppering her with questions, but she wouldn't say any more—just that she would make sure Justin's cardiologist knew we were waiting to talk to her.

It was time for the nurses to change shifts, but I didn't want to leave. My mind was full of questions and I did not want to risk missing Justin's doctor. But they asked us to leave, so we stepped out into the waiting room, afraid to venture any further. It was still too early to call family, and we really had very little to tell them—just a repeat of what the nurse had said. Nothing concrete and no real answers for the many questions we knew they would have.

I didn't feel well, so I ate a few crackers from a well-stocked supply that friends and family had brought. Neither of us wanted any breakfast. We just wanted answers. We sat as patiently as we could in the waiting room until we knew the shift change must be over, and then we headed back to Justin's bedside. When we arrived, we were disappointed and angry to learn that Justin's cardiologist had been there and had ordered an EEG and a couple of other tests but had left without seeking us out or speaking to us. The nurse now on duty said she felt certain that Justin's doctor would talk to us as soon as she had the results of the tests she had ordered.

Robby spoke to the charge nurse on the floor, but he wasn't able to get any answers. We would just have to wait. He went to make phone calls to family, and I stayed with Justin. As I sat by Justin's bed, I tried to take his small hand, which was strapped to a wrist board, in mine, but his arms were tightly bent and I couldn't lower his arm to his side. I mentioned it to the nurse, and soon the charge nurse was beside Justin's bed examining his rigid body. His legs as well as his feet were now stiff and straight while both arms were bent in and tight against his chest.

A little while later, a technician arrived and began affixing electric leads all over Justin's head. The leads were held on by what appeared to be little wads of yellow putty. He told us we could stay while he attached the electrodes, but once the EEG machine arrived, we would have to leave because the machine would leave little space in the tiny cubical. The technician was very kind and tried to assure us that the results of the test would be available to Justin's doctor very quickly.

By the time the EEG machine had arrived on the floor, family members had begun to gather in the waiting room. My parents were there with Jacob and Jerrod. The unanswered questions and ominous feeling in the pit of my stomach collided with a sudden rush of homesickness when my little boys came running. It took all the emotional restraint I could muster to keep back the tears that threatened to spill from brimming eyes. I didn't want anyone to see me cry or let go of my optimistic outlook. If I could keep a positive attitude and ignore the possibility that things might not turn out well . . . if I could hold tightly to my faith that God would take care of both Justin and our family . . . if I did not waver or show any doubt . . . then I felt certain all would be okay in the end. I would not allow myself to think otherwise. I just had to be patient. Every time someone asked if I was all right, I would say I was just disappointed in another setback because I was ready to go home.

By early afternoon the waiting room was full of family and close friends waiting with us for news. Our phone calls to family that morning with the news that Justin was displaying signs of brain damage had led to announcements and prayer requests in several churches that morning, and everyone was anxious for more substantial information.

Robby and I took turns with grandparents and immediate family keeping a constant vigil at Justin's bedside. Finally, that afternoon Justin's cardiologist arrived and stepped out into the back hall of the ICU room to talk with us.

"Justin is in a coma," she told us simply. "It will be difficult to determine what caused the damage. As you know, open-heart surgery always comes with the risk of blood clots or stroke. You'll recall the papers you signed before admitting Justin for surgery that explained the many risks inherent to valve replacement procedures." She speculated that the damage could have occurred the night after surgery, and it just took several days for the swelling on his brain to build up enough pressure to display any symptoms. Perhaps that could explain why he had difficulty coming off of the ventilator the day before. There were any number of things that could have occurred, she reiterated. She concluded it would not be possible to tell what exactly had caused the damage nor could she give us any indication as to the extent of the damage. She told us Justin would likely remain comatose until the swelling subsided. There was no way of knowing the extent of the brain damage until he was conscious. As she stood up to leave, she summarized, "At this point, there is nothing you can do but wait."

We repeated the doctor's report to the family and friends waiting for news. I still could not grasp the gravity of the situation. Justin was in a coma, but he was alive. We just had to wait until the swelling on his brain subsided, and then he would wake up.

My mother began to cry and I felt at a loss as to how to console her. Robby's dad asked if the doctors were certain he would eventually wake up. The thought that Justin might not wake up had not occurred to me. The ominous cloud of despair that had lifted slightly when we finally had some information about Justin's condition quickly returned.

Someone led our group in prayer. Later, someone else brought food, but the day passed slowly without any change in Justin's condition.

I took turns holding Jacob and Jerrod in my lap that day, asking them about their week. They were both talkative, but Jacob asked in his high-pitched little voice, "Mama, when are we going to go home to our house?"

"I don't know, sweetheart." I pulled him close and kissed the top of his blond head. "Can you be a big boy and stay with Nana tonight?"

"Yes, but when are we going home to our house? I want to go home to our house."

His pleading little voice made it hard to contain my

tears, but I smiled and tried to reassure him. "It won't be too long and we'll all go home together. We just need to wait until Justin gets well."

"Will Justin go home with us?"

"Yes, Justin will come home with us," I said, hoping that saying it aloud would make it true.

"Is he in the hospital room? Why can't we go in there? I want to play with his masher truck."

"Well, Justin is very sick, so we can't go in there right now. He took his masher truck apart, but when he is better maybe you can ask him to make another one." I talked with as much optimism as I could muster.

It was obvious Jacob missed his big brother and the routine of home. Jacob was already learning to keep his emotions in check, but his blue eyes glistened with tears when he realized he was not going home yet and would once again leave with grandparents. Jerrod, still a baby, seemed content with the situation. It was difficult for me to watch them leave, knowing it might be another week before I would see them again.

As the day drew to a close, visitors began to say their good-byes. Robby and I were left to spend another long night among the stark walls of the ICU waiting room.

⌒ Chapter 7 ⌒

Trials He Chooses

O Lord, I cry out to you. I will keep on pleading day by day.
O Lord, why do you reject me? Why do you turn your face from me?
Psalm 88:13-14

The next few days were uneventful and empty. Justin's condition remained unchanged. Every day someone came to visit and check on us. My mother took our dirty clothes and returned them clean and laundered. We knew that many people were praying for us back home. I was grateful for the prayers since my own prayers seemed empty and hollow. I had brought my Bible to the hospital, but I had not read it. I found I could not focus on the words that had brought me comfort in times past, so eventually I quit trying. I told myself that once Justin got into a room, it would be easier to read and I would have more privacy to spend time in God's Word. I clung to the hope that once Justin was transferred to a room, this awful waiting for him to regain consciousness would finally be over.

Although there wasn't any apparent change in Justin's condition, his doctor ordered an EEG to be run regularly. We did not see his doctor during those long quiet days, but we were told that we would be notified of any change in Justin's condition. Two days into the second week following surgery, Justin's cardiologist and a pediatric neurologist she had consulted asked to meet with us in the little chapel where we had sat and prayed with the hospital chaplain that night after surgery. I listened numbly as the neurologist explained that according to the EEG, Justin was only functioning with minimal brain stem activity and that no other activity had been recorded even though the swelling on his brain had somewhat subsided.

"I think there are some decisions you and your wife need to discuss," the neurologist said to Robby, avoiding eye contact with me. "Justin's ventilator is still on full capacity, but it may be simply keeping his body alive. This is not a decision you need to make right away. Children can be very resilient, and so I suggest we give Justin a few more days. But if there is no improvement over the weekend . . . well, then I think we will need to talk again and decide if keeping his body alive is the best option for Justin and your family." The doctor's face was grave as he rose to leave. "We'll give you and your wife some time. Feel free to use this room as long as you like and just close the door when you leave." As they left, he added, "I'm really sorry."

I felt as though I couldn't breathe. How could we make *that* decision?

Left alone to discuss this grave news, our primary topic of discussion was whether we should tell our parents that we may have to face this awful decision. We couldn't seem to discuss the topic beyond that, and I was thankful for the cushion of three days. I hoped we would not have to make the decision. I was so tired and homesick, and it seemed as though there was no end to this terrible ordeal—but I could not imagine going home without Justin. I could not believe he was gone. Somewhere in that little body, the spirit of an energetic, talkative, and intelligent little boy still had to exist.

The words did not come easy, but somehow we told those we felt had a right to know. Reverend Bruce Keller came to visit us many times during that long stay. Brother Bruce, as we referred to him, had married Robby and me and had been a dear friend of our family for a long time. His grandson was one of Justin's friends. On Friday, as we prepared to wait out that long weekend, Brother Bruce arrived to offer his prayers and support. I coveted his prayers, but as he prayed, I was horrified to hear him say, "Lord, we pray for this child's complete healing, but we trust that your purpose will be accomplished in all things. So we pray for lasting strength for this family to endure whatever trials you choose to lay before them."

Strength to endure whatever trials HE CHOOSES to lay before us? *What did he mean by that?* I just wanted Justin complete and whole and I wanted this trial to be over—surely *that* was the Lord's will. I couldn't imagine why God would choose not to heal Justin if he truly heard the prayers of his people and was concerned at all about the events of our lives. Why would he allow Justin to suffer? Why would God *choose* to put us through this trial? Certainly it must be Satan that brought this evil on us.

However, this last thought troubled me. If Satan did this to Justin, then where was God? Didn't God have the power to prevent this? And if so, why didn't he?

It all just seemed so unfair. I had thought Justin's surgery was a trial that would bring God glory. I knew I wasn't perfect, but I was a good person. I professed Christ as my savior and Lord, and I thought he would use our faith as a witness to others in the hospital. In my mind, the only outcome that would bring God glory would be Justin's complete recovery . . . but Brother Bruce asked that the Lord give us lasting strength to endure whatever trials HE might choose to walk us through. It was very confusing. I just needed the strength to get through the next couple of weeks—surely this trial would be over by then. How much longer could it be? Why would he even need to pray that the Lord's will be done when it was so clear that anything short of a miraculous healing could not be God's will? I was disappointed. I had leaned on this great man in hopes he would strengthen my faith, and instead I was left with more questions, more confusion.

Saturday morning I woke early and once again washed my hair in the sink of the ladies restroom directly across the hall from the ICU waiting room. Then began what was becoming my usual morning routine of changing clothes, applying makeup, and brushing my teeth before going to see Justin. Although performing my morning toiletries in the public restroom was becoming routine, it still made me uncomfortable and I tried to get there early to avoid the company of anyone who may need to use the facilities.

Justin had been in the ICU for ten days, which meant we had spent the previous ten nights in the hospital. I could not help but think that we should be in a room in the children's wing, that Justin should be awake and talking by now, and that we should be making plans to go home. Instead, we were still sleeping in the ICU waiting room while Justin was still listed in critical care. I was surprised to discover how much these thoughts angered me.

When I arrived in the ICU, the nurse at Justin's bedside was anxious to see me. "Good news! Justin's blood gas reports this morning came back very high, and the pulmonologist is going to speak to his doctor about possibly lowering the rate of his ventilator. It seems possible that Justin may be breathing a bit!" Her excitement at such a tiny hint of improvement had my hopes soaring.

We never saw his cardiologist, but another EEG was ordered. Later that morning, Justin's neurologist arrived with news. "It's still inconclusive, but Justin's latest EEG this morning seems to indicate that perhaps there is some improvement and a slight increase in brain activity. As I said before, children can be resilient. Given this change in his condition, I don't recommend that we make any major decisions regarding his care for at least another week."

We had been spared the trial of making that awful decision about Justin's life support. Later Robby asked me how I would have decided, but I couldn't say—I honestly didn't know. The thought was still too disturbing to even consider. That was a trial God chose not to walk us through.

⌐ Chapter 8 ⌐

Defeated Hope

Hope deferred makes the heart sick.
Proverbs 13:12

Although we did not have to decide about Justin's life support, we would soon be facing another decision: If Justin were to remain on a ventilator, he would need to have a tracheotomy done to prevent damage to his vocal cords. A tracheotomy would also make it easier on Justin when and if he could eventually be weaned off the ventilator. The pulmonologist said he would give us some time to think about it and would discuss it with Justin's neurologist and cardiologist.

As the weekend passed, the doctors were able to lower Justin's ventilator rate a little, but they proceeded cautiously. On Monday the decision was made to perform a tracheotomy, and the procedure was done quickly. Justin's sensitive skin was chapped and raw from the tape that had held the ventilator tube in place. With the help of a nurse, I gently cleaned away the sticky remains of the tape and applied some moisturizer to his red cheeks. We also gently sponged his little body, working around the tubes and electronic leads that still remained, and spread a clean hospital gown over him. There had been so very little I could do for him, it felt good to care for him once again. It was nice to see him without the ventilator tube, but even without the tube, his face was swollen and puffy. He did not look at all like the same little boy.

Although the electrodes from the EEG were still attached to his head and he still had an IV, an arterial line, and a subclavian port, both of his chest drainage tubes and his external pacemaker had been removed. His catheter had also been removed, and he now wore a diaper. The sight of a diaper on his unconscious little body mortified me for his sake, and I tried to make sure his hospital gown covered it completely.

Although his legs and feet were massaged several times throughout the day, they remained rigid. His arms were still drawn up tight against his chest. But with the tracheotomy in place, the doctors were willing to try to lower his ventilator a little more, and he seemed to respond by breathing a little on his own. It was an undetectable response, but I clung to the hope that he would soon be breathing on his own—the first step toward recovery.

Another week passed slowly by. Justin's body continued to heal from his surgery despite a setback from a staph infection, but he remained unresponsive and deeply comatose. Every day I would sit by his bedside, reading and talking to him while watching carefully for any sign of a response. His progress toward breathing on his own was very slow and we were told he may stabilize at a lower rate but remain unable to breathe on his own without assistance. The nurses encouraged us to continue talking to Justin and reassuring him, but the doctors—when we saw them—offered little encouragement. In fact, they said very little at all.

It was almost two weeks after Justin had slipped into a coma before he made any real response. Aside from some improvement on his EEG and a slight increase in his respiratory rate, he remained stiff and unresponsive. As part of his routine care, respiratory therapists regularly suctioned his airways through his trach. One morning while being suctioned, Justin began to cough as his body attempted to clear his air passages.

There was an air of excitement among the nurses at this first indication that Justin was beginning to respond to outside stimulation. Robby and I were also excited. We spent the rest of the day earnestly talking to Justin, asking him to open his eyes, wiggle his fingers, move his toes—anything to indicate he could hear and respond to us.

Although Justin did not respond or do anything we pleaded for him to do, he did continue to cough when he was suctioned. Soon he was also making an attempt at a cry, though the sound of his voice was blocked by the trachea tube. His nurse was very compassionate as she explained to us how painful it was for heart patients to cough following surgery. My heart ached to think he was in pain and a silent cry was his only means of communicating it.

I had not left the hospital since Justin had been re-intubated. Robby made a couple of quick trips home to check on the house and take care of a few things, but we both spent our nights at the hospital, sleeping in the ICU waiting room.

We finally left the hospital to attend my younger brother's

graduation ceremony while our dear friend, Brother Bruce, attended Justin's bedside. I was anxious about leaving, but it was nice to get away for bit. Our hometown had set up a trust fund for Justin at the local bank, and Justin remained on the prayer list at several local churches. But it seemed strange to realize that outside the hospital, life continued. Friends and family had gone back to their normal lives. They went to work, attended school, and planned for special events while our lives were on hold—waiting for the day when Justin would wake up, get better, and come home.

We arrived at the graduation ceremony just before it began, so there was not much time to talk or answer inquires from well-meaning friends. However, following the ceremony, Robby and I found we were suddenly bombarded with questions from concerned friends and distant relatives.

"I heard your little boy went into a coma after his surgery. Is he conscious yet?"

"Is that a common complication of open-heart surgery? I've never heard of someone slipping into a coma after surgery before. What caused that?"

"I heard your little boy is still in the hospital. Do you know when he's going to get to come home?"

"How's Justin? We heard he was still in the hospital. Is there anything we can get for you? Would he like some coloring books?"

It had not occurred to me that I would have to discuss Justin's condition with so many people. I didn't know what to say—I wasn't even sure myself what had happened or why he was in a coma. Nor could I say what his prognosis was since the doctors had been very vague about their expectations for his recovery.

When we mentioned the recent improvements in his ventilator rate and his response to suctioning, we were met with either blank looks as people tried to fathom how that could be an improvement, or with sympathetic smiles. What had filled me with hope and excitement now left me hopeless and defeated as I saw myself grasping at the smallest improvements that offered little real hope at all. I felt overwhelmed and could not wait to head back to the hospital. Robby and I spoke little on the drive back, both lost in our own thoughts and struggling with unanswered questions.

☞ Chapter 9 ☜

Abrupt Reality

That is what the Scriptures mean when they say, "No eye has seen, no ear has heard, and no mind has imagined, what God has prepared for those who love him."
1 Corinthians 2:9

May was quickly passing, and Justin had been in the ICU for almost a month. We had seen very little of his cardiologist after that first week, but she was still writing his orders and directing his care. However, when Justin started coughing and responding to pain, she began to once more make her presence available to us. She even introduced the idea of moving him out of the ICU and into the rehabilitation unit.

My only exposure to someone emerging from a coma had come from television and stories I had read. Each case always involved someone instantly waking, and no one had explained to us this was not generally the case. In fact, no one had explained what we could expect at all . . . either best or worst case scenario. We were so uninformed we didn't even know what questions to ask. I had no reference to help me comprehend what brain damage was or how it might be manifested. I had been excited when Justin began responding to pain, but I was still waiting for the day he would open his eyes and try to talk. I was soon to face the abrupt reality of brain damage.

Justin's cardiologist set up a time for the director of the hospital's rehab unit to come down to the ICU and see Justin, evaluate him, give us a tour of the rehab unit, and explain to us what kind of therapy he might receive and what we could expect once he arrived in the unit.

The director was very kind. She met us at Justin's bedside and smiled compassionately, which was a nice change from the distance of the other doctors. Justin's hands were tightly clenched in fists and sharply turned in at the wrist; his arms were pulled in tight to his chest, and we were no longer able to extend them. The muscles in his legs and feet were rigid, and his toes were pointed sharply down. As the rehab director gently felt his tight muscles, she explained to us about contractures and said she would send therapists down to the ICU to begin working to stretch Justin's contracted muscles even before he was admitted to the rehab unit. Given the current condition of his contractures, she felt serial casting would be the best way to begin. She explained that this was a procedure that would help stretch the tightened muscles in his limbs by extending the tightened joint a little at a time until the muscle relaxed in the extended position.

She also explained to us that many times—especially when severe brain damage has occurred—people emerge slowly from a coma over several weeks or even months, and that Justin's response to pain was hopefully the first stages of that process. I listened and tried to comprehend the meaning in her words when she told us it would be difficult to tell at what point the process would plateau, but that she hoped Justin still had a long way to go before he reached that point. She hoped that since he was a child, he would continue to improve and learn for many years. She explained that the process of rehabilitation begins as therapists try to retrain the working areas of the brain to assume some of the work once done by the damaged areas.

Her words gave us hope as she told us that although there is never a good age for a person to suffer brain damage, Justin was a good candidate for recovery since he was old enough to have learned how to walk and talk but still young enough that his brain might be easily retrained.

After our calm and somewhat reassuring talk with the director, I was completely unprepared for what I saw in the rehab unit. Almost immediately after we entered the unit, two therapists came down the hall wheeling a gurney with a young girl. She looked to be about thirteen or fourteen, but she was making wailing sounds like an infant and drooling from one side of her mouth. Her face was contorted and drawn to one side and reminded me of an elderly stroke victim. She seemed to be uncontrollably flailing her arms, but her movements were stiff and jerky as though she were pulling her arms in and some unseen force was jerking them straight again. Her clenched fists looked eerily similar to Justin's, although her wrists were bent back toward the top of her arm rather than bent inward. While one leg remained bent at the knee and drawn up close to her torso, the other she would pull up toward her body and then suddenly stiffen and kick out with bare toes pointed—a gesture she repeated in a rhythmic pattern.

Our tour guide must have noticed me staring at the young girl as she was wheeled down the hall. Before I could ask, she gently explained that the girl had suffered a seizure in which she quit breathing for quite some time. Before I could stop myself, I asked, "Was she normal before that?"

She gently smiled and replied softly, "Yes." Then she quickly added, "But she is making real progress and has even managed to say a few words."

I remembered nothing of the rest of the tour. I could not take my mind off the girl. Was that what we were facing? I had envisioned Justin sitting up in bed, talking to his nurses. When we were told he might have brain damage, I had thought that he might have some memory loss or perhaps have some difficulty with his fine motor skills. His clutched fists and bent wrists made me envision him exercising his fingers and perhaps relearning how to hold a cup or utensils. But the sight of that young girl had abruptly opened my eyes to a whole new world—a world I had never imagined might exist for my son or for our family. It was a world to which I had never been exposed and barely knew existed. I numbly followed the coordinator as she led us around the rehab facilities.

Once we were back in the ICU, I quickly excused myself and blindly made my way to the ladies room. It was empty and I shut myself in a stall. Tears that I had long held in check began to fall in a steady flow and drip from my chin. I heaved silent sobs for a few moments and then tried desperately to regain my composure. When I felt I could finally breathe steadily, I made my way to the sink and tried to bathe my eyes and wash away the evidence of my tears.

While I was trying to conceal the evidence of my lost composure, an elderly black woman entered. I recognized her as one of the custodians for the ICU. Though she rarely spoke, her eyes always had a gentle look of compassion. When she saw me desperately trying to squelch the flow of tears that refused to stop, she touched my shoulder and said gently, "Honey, you have every reason to cry. Crying don't mean you've given up and it don't mean God has left you or that little boy of yours neither."

Her words brought on an onslaught of fresh tears; they were exactly the truth that I needed to hear.

By refusing to let myself cry or even acknowledge that Justin's situation looked grim, I was desperately trying to hold on to my faith. I still could not believe that the God I trusted would allow something so bad to happen if he did not ultimately plan a happy ending. Surely that's why we were here: to give evidence to God's healing power. I clung desperately to a belief that God would suddenly—or maybe even slowly—completely heal Justin. Leaving her cleaning cart, God's messenger quietly stepped out of the restroom to give me a few more minutes alone.

Later that night as I tried in vain to sleep, I realized how sheltered my young life had been. Somehow I had lived twenty-five years without realizing such hardship and heartache existed. How could God leave Justin in the same condition as the young girl in rehab? How could God leave that young girl in her present state? She must also have family and parents who were heartbroken to watch their daughter revert to an almost infantile state. I thought of the family who had lost their son several years earlier, and I realized I had not resolved (and still could not resolve) an issue that was suddenly threatening the core of my faith. It was an issue I had refused to think about then and did not want to face now—how a good God could allow such bad things to happen.

Surely these horrible tragedies happened only to people who didn't serve him or to those who had committed some horrific hidden sin. Growing up in a conservative church in West Texas, a part of the country once deemed the "Bible belt" of the nation, I had always been taught that God blesses those who serve him—those who are good—and he allows hardship and tragedy to befall those who have either fallen away or never acknowledged him. But I hadn't committed some awful sin. I had always tried to be good. Wasn't that enough to deserve blessings?

My head was pounding and I did not want to wrestle with these thoughts. I resolved to push such questions aside and hold on to my faith in a good God who would heal my son if only I would believe. To allow myself to doubt might threaten the security of Justin's healing. It might also threaten the foundation of my faith, which I felt had already been cracked—and I was desperately trying to mend the fissure.

Chapter 10

Long Lonely Days and Nights

Save me, O God, for the floodwaters are up to my neck.
Deeper and deeper I sink into the mire; I can't find a foothold.
I am in deep water, and the floods overwhelm me. I am
exhausted from crying for help; my throat is parched. My
eyes are swollen with weeping, waiting for my God to help me.
Psalm 69:1-3

When June arrived, Justin was still in the ICU and still on a ventilator, but he was breathing a little more on his own and his respiration rate on the vent had been lowered. He was not only responding to pain but also was now silently crying, or rather screaming, whenever he was suctioned or moved. He had become very sensitive to touch and cried as though in pain whenever he was moved or repositioned. His hands and arms were still tightly contracted. Although his therapist could sometimes get the muscles in his legs to relax after a session of deep massage, they would instantly stiffen the minute he was touched again. His feet remained extended and they now turned inward. There were plans to begin serial casting on him to reduce his contractures, but it had not yet been started. The nurses and therapists were unable to detect any pattern of a sleep and wake cycle, as there never seemed to be a time when Justin was relaxed and asleep nor was he ever completely conscious. We were told this indicated he was still semi-comatose; however, we later learned that severe brain damage can result in a permanently disrupted sleep-wake cycle. Occasionally, he would open his eyes, but he never appeared to focus on anything or anyone, and his pupils remained large and dilated for several minutes before responding to the light.

However, despite his seemingly unresponsive state, I was sometimes able to calm his silent cries by singing to him softly: "If you listen you can hear the voice of Jesus whisper in your ear, 'I'll never leave you or forsake you dear; I'm right here with you, you've nothing to fear.' Jesus whispers in your ear."

Everyone agreed that Justin obviously recognized my voice. Occasionally, he would even open his eyes in response to my voice. Although he did not appear to focus on me or anything in particular, it gave me reason to hope.

One day while I was talking and singing softly to him, Justin's nurse suggested that I try rocking him to see if his body would respond positively to the firmer touch of being held and the motion of rocking. I looked at my son, who was still connected to an IV by the port located just below his collarbone. He also had a tracheotomy tube connected to the respirator and his O_2 stats were being monitored by a small sensor connected to his finger. Although his connections appeared to be very minimal compared to earlier weeks, they still seemed to be more than I could manage. The thought of holding him in that condition had never occurred to me. In fact, I had never even thought of holding him at all. Justin was the eldest of three—soon to be four—children, and I had not held or carried him in a long time. He was always my helper and usually carried something for me or held my hand when we went somewhere. He was the one who stood beside the rocking chair and looked on while I rocked his little brothers. He was the one who cuddled up close and held the book while I held his brothers and read. It had been a long time since I had held him in my lap.

As I looked at him with uncertainty, I did not want to admit that the thought of holding him made me feel awkward and uncomfortable. I was afraid to hold him. But the nurse insisted and had soon procured a large rocking chair and moved the bed over in his tiny cubical to make room for the chair in the cramped space.

I obediently sat in the chair while she and another nurse maneuvered Justin's tubing and gently lifted his stiff body into my lap. Justin protested at the touch with silent screams and I wasn't sure I could keep his stiff body in what little remained of my lap beyond the bulge of my pregnant belly. But his nurses and I managed to bend him slightly at the waist and at the knees. His arms remained tightly bent and compressed against his chest, and I found he had no head control. The increased muscle tone that caused certain muscles to contract because of the brain damage affected the muscles in his neck, causing him to pull his head forward toward his chest, so it was difficult to keep him from bumping his chin on his clutched fists. I was concerned he would compromise the airflow through his "trach," so I desperately tried to hold his head up against the tight muscles pulling it forward.

Justin felt like a stranger in my lap. He didn't even feel like a child, but something completely foreign. The physical and emotional strain soon made me feel sick. Embarrassed to say anything to his well-meaning nurses, I tried to control my nausea as long as possible. I rocked for a few minutes, but it soon threatened to overwhelm me, so I told his nurses I really needed to get up. As they lifted him back into his bed, I managed to slip out around them and down the hall just in time. When I returned, the rocking chair had been moved out and nothing else was said about the incident, nor was it again suggested that I hold him while he remained in the ICU.

Justin spent thirty-one days in the ICU and Robby and I slept in the ICU waiting room thirty-one nights. Finally, Justin was moved to a room in the new children's wing of the hospital. The wing had been under construction when we had come into the hospital, so Justin was one of the first patients on the floor. It was spacious for a hospital room, and it had the luxury of a private bathroom complete with a shower! It had a padded bench seat that doubled as a bed and stored extra pillows and blankets underneath the seat. There were a TV and a recliner and a small closet where I could store our things. It felt like a palace.

That first night on the children's wing after Justin was settled and calm, a children's nurse brought me a hot cup of tea and some crackers and cheese. "Here dear, I figure you missed your supper in the move and I thought you may like something to eat and a hot cup of tea to calm your nerves. I'm sure all this has been hard on you," she said as she sat the tray down beside Justin's bed. "We'll order you a guest tray to be delivered with the patient's meals." She retrieved blankets and a pillow from the padded bench. "You should try to get some sleep. Hopefully, you'll be comfortable here."

The thought of actually sleeping on something designed for that purpose and having access to a shower the next morning was almost overwhelming. I found myself unable to both thank her and retain my composure, so as tears spilled from my brimming eyes, I put the cup to my lips to give myself just a second to gain control before responding. She seemed to understand and slipped quietly out of the room. Alone with Justin, I struggled for several minutes before I was able to stop the flow of tears. I was so exhausted. I was thankful to finally be out of the ICU, but I was also very homesick and lonely.

Robby worked as a farmhand, and his boss had been supportive and had allowed him to take more than three weeks off while Justin was listed in critical condition. However, it was planting season and Robby had gone back to work by the end of May. He stayed at the house or at his parents' during the week since our boys were there, visited the hospital each Saturday, and returned home on Sunday night. The once steady stream of visitors had slowly trickled down, and now most of our guests came only on the weekends.

Unfortunately, Justin's stay in the children's unit was relatively short. Within two weeks we were moved into the rehab unit. His room in rehab was smaller, but it still had a private bathroom with a shower and room for a cot. During his last week in the ICU and while he was on the children's floor, a physical therapist came daily to work with his tightly contracted arms, wrists, and feet but had made little progress toward loosening his tight muscles. Justin's nurses and I had spent long hours rubbing his arms, hands, face, and legs in an attempt to desensitize him to touch. Although he was still very sensitive, he was no longer screaming at the slightest touch.

His eyes were open more. Though unable to track objects, he did appear to be focusing and had less of a glazed expression. His eyes opened wide whenever he heard something familiar, making it obvious that he recognized certain voices, music, books, and movies. His pupils also responded more quickly to light.

Justin still had not developed a regular sleep-wake cycle, but there were times when he was obviously asleep and other times when he was more conscious and somewhat aware of his surroundings. During the day, he seemed to nap easily, drifting in and out of sleep throughout the day; however, toward evening, he would become incredibly irritable and would often spend several hours screaming inaudibly because he still had a trach. I spent hours beside his bed trying in vain to comfort him. During those times, his muscles became rigid and his sensitivity to touch seemed to increase. Even singing seemed to do little to comfort him. I was afraid that his efforts to cry with the trach may damage his vocal cords, but since he was not yet fully conscious, his doctor would not prescribe anything to calm or sedate him. His neurologist told us it was a condition called neurological crying or neuro-irritability and that it was unlikely Justin was in pain. I was never certain of his assumption. It seemed to me that his stiff and contracted muscles and his sensitivity to touch might actually be very painful to him. However, it was difficult to determine if his muscles stiffened and became tighter, causing him pain and evoking the screaming episodes . . . or if the screaming episodes caused his body to stiffen. Whatever the cause, it was almost unbearable to witness, and I was helpless to calm him.

After the first week of Justin's hospital stay, Grandpa

and Mamma kept Jacob and Jerrod most of the week since my parents both had to go back to work. Papa and Nana kept them on the weekends—often bringing them to the hospital to visit.

However, once Justin was admitted to rehab in late June and school was out for the summer, Nana (who worked at the school) was able to help more with the boys. I had not spent the night at home since Justin's surgery and had left the hospital only for my brother's graduation and my doctor appointments. I was torn between staying with Justin and a deep longing for home and family. Although my due date was still a couple of months away, several family members and friends—including my doctor—thought I needed a break from the hospital. So my mother, my mother-in-law, and I began to rotate between Justin and the boys. Nana and Mamma would each stay two days and two nights a week with Justin while I stayed home with Jacob and Jerrod. Then I would stay three days and three nights with Justin while they took turns keeping the boys—and so began the long days of rehabilitation. While I was at home, I would miss Justin terribly and think about him constantly. While I was at the hospital, I missed home and my little boys immensely. I felt torn between two worlds and longed for the day when we would all be together once more.

Justin continued to make small improvements. As soon as he was settled in rehab, his therapists began serial casting on his arms and feet. Soon they were able to fully extend his arms. Once they had reduced the contractures, Justin began to move his right arm at the shoulder and the elbow. His movements were awkward and seemed to be instinctive rather than purposeful, but we all rejoiced to see him wrinkle his nose and swipe at his face in an effort to scratch his nose.

He still had a trach, but he needed very little assistance from the ventilator and was now able to be disconnected from it for short periods. A gastric feeding tube had been inserted before he left the ICU, and his therapists—with the consent of his gastroenterologist—had begun the process of weaning him from a continuous g-tube feed to a nightly g-tube feed. He still could not track with his eyes or communicate in any way. He was incontinent and he struggled with head control and drooling. Although he would open his eyes and appeared to be listening intently at times, he never smiled.

I found myself struggling to remember the sound of his voice. I wished I could read his thoughts as I tried to interpret his cries and his limited movements. I prayed God would speed the day when Justin would once again speak and communicate. I continually prayed for strength to accept and handle any lingering physical limitations Justin might be left with while I begged God to quickly restore his ability to speak.

Though I didn't realize it at the time, my prayers were my way of bartering with God. If he would just give me the strength to handle any physical handicaps Justin might have... if I did my part and was willing to accept imperfection . . . then perhaps God would allow the little boy I knew must exist somewhere deep inside to express himself once more. I pleaded with God to let Justin maintain his full cognitive abilities. I begged him to restore the bright, intelligent little boy even if Justin had to live within the confines of a twisted body. I promised to give God all the glory for his healing and all the praise for bringing us through such a difficult situation—another attempt to barter. It never occurred to me that all the praise and all the glory were God's regardless. He didn't need me to lavish praise from a heart that felt entitled to some good because of my extreme effort to accept a gift I perceived to be less than perfect.

⌒ Chapter 11 ⌒

Home at Last

Plans succeed through good counsel;
don't go to war without wise advice.
Proverbs 20:18

On July 23, a bright ray of sunlight entered our darkened world: a beautiful, healthy baby girl was born to our family. She was five weeks premature, but unlike the boys, her lungs appeared to be fully developed and she did not experience any difficulties from her early arrival.

Just days after her birth, I was once again at Justin's bedside, this time with Jennifer in tow. I was nursing Jennifer, so I couldn't leave her with anyone—not that I wanted to leave my new baby for even a few hours. Now that I was no longer pregnant, I was determined to learn how to care for Justin. I was ready for Justin to come home; I felt I was about to reach the limit of my abilities to withstand hospital living. I did not think I could nurse and care for a new baby while staying with Justin in the rehab wing for long, nor was I willing to give up my responsibilities to either of them.

Justin's breathing had continued to improve. The week Jennifer was born, his doctors had ordered a Passy-Muir valve for his tracheotomy since he could now be disconnected from the ventilator and connected only to oxygen for most of the day. With the valve, his screams were now audible though we did not use it all the time as episodes of inconsolable crying continued on a regular basis.

Although it was much worse at night, Justin was still irritable throughout the day due in part to his sensitivity to touch and his inability to communicate, but I was learning to discern some of his cries and was often able to attend his needs or comfort him. While I stayed with him in the children's unit, I learned how to change him and dress him despite the high muscle tone that made his limbs stiff and the job difficult. We spent some of the money friends and family had given us on new clothes for Justin: knit tops that stretched easily, sweat suits, and relaxed-fit jeans (it just did not seem as if he were dressed unless he wore jeans). Every morning, I would change him and dress him. There was something comforting and routine about getting him dressed each morning that made me feel as though he were actually recovering.

The brain damage had caused some of Justin's muscles and tendons to remain loose without any tone or control while creating increased or high tone in other muscles and tendons. After Jennifer's birth, I learned how to bend Justin's legs and help his muscles relax and how to gently stretch and flex his extremities—applying slow and steady pressure until I felt his muscles relax and loosen. Repeating this exercise several times a day would help stretch his tendons and prevent contractures. And despite protests from others regarding my health and recent delivery, I soon learned how to lift and transfer Justin to my lap or to a stroller-type wheelchair. The more I cared for him, the more comfortable I became with his care. He no longer felt like the stranger I once held in the ICU. I had also learned how to operate the pump for his g-tube and how to clean and care for his trach and the IV port on his chest (it was no longer in use but kept in place as a precautionary measure).

His therapists had worked to get his g-tube feeding schedule down from a continuous feed to a nightly feed, and soon Justin was no longer attached to the ventilator or his feeding pump during the day. This gave him more mobility and his therapists were able to take him from his room to the PT room for therapy, where they could begin working with him on upper-body control and balance. Since he still lacked sufficient upper-body control to support himself in a traditional wheelchair, Justin was wheeled from room to room in a large reclining umbrella-style stroller, but he was now mobile.

All these changes convinced me I could care for Justin at home just as easily as I could at the hospital—without being torn away from the rest of my family. Caring for Jennifer at home would be so much easier than trying to take her to the hospital with me where she had to sleep in her infant seat.

One night when I was home and our evening felt almost routine except for the void Justin's absence created—especially for me—I approached Robby. "I want to bring Justin home."

"I don't know, Sheila." Robby was skeptical. "I don't know if we're ready to care for him yet. Maybe when he gets a little better and he can tell us what he needs and where he hurts." His voice trailed off and neither of us would allow ourselves to consider that day might not come. We both clung to the hope that Justin would continue to improve and would eventually talk again.

"But, I don't think it would be any harder for me to care for him here as it is for me to keep going back and forth." I persisted. "It is so hard for me to take care of Jennifer when I'm at the hospital with Justin."

"I know going back and forth is getting hard on my mother and your mother too." Robby hesitated and then continued. "Have you . . . um . . . considered . . . or thought about leaving Justin there some by himself?" He quickly added, "I'm sure they would take care of him or they wouldn't have told us we could leave him if we needed to."

I was surprised and hurt by his suggestion. I knew Robby was not as familiar or comfortable with Justin's care as I was since he had only spent three weeks at the hospital at the very beginning. I also knew he was uncomfortable with Justin. But it did not occur to me that Justin still felt very much a stranger to his father - as much as he had felt a stranger to me that day in the rocking chair. "Robby," I said quietly as I tried to steady my voice and calm my emotions, "they just let him scream at night and don't even try to comfort him or see if maybe he is hurting somewhere. I can take care of him, but I can't leave him up there without someone to watch over him and care for him."

"Okay, Sheila, if you think you can handle it, I'll support you. I want our family to be together again too."

The next week, Robby came with me to the hospital and we spoke to the rehab coordinator and the hospital administrator about taking Justin home. I was surprised when we met with resistance. While the hospital administrator said she would not release him without signed consent from his doctor, the rehab coordinator reluctantly agreed to consult with his admitting doctor (his cardiologist) and the other doctors and therapists involved in his care. Within a few days, a meeting was arranged to discuss Justin's progress, his prognosis, and the possibility of releasing him from the hospital. It was a difficult meeting. I understood that Justin needed to continue intensive therapy and we were willing to negotiate arrangements regarding his therapy, but I needed to be home at night and I needed Justin to be home with me. However, no one in that room aside from us felt that Justin should be released from the hospital.

I felt their concerns were not really based on Justin's needs. All agreed I had shown I was capable of caring for him, so I could not understand their reluctance to release him to our care. I had been handling the majority of his care and never left him unattended. While the nurses and staff on the rehab floor made routine checks, they left him alone for long periods. So when it was suggested again that we consider leaving Justin unattended during the week and in the care of the hospital staff to relieve his grandmothers and me of the unnecessary burden we had taken on ourselves, my face flushed red hot with anger. However, I managed to calmly state that I would not even consider their suggestion because of the quality of care I had witnessed. In the end, it was agreed that Justin would be discharged on a one-day pass at the end of the week. Then the team would meet again if we were still intent on having him permanently discharged.

On August 7, 1992, we brought Justin home to spend the day. It was his sixth birthday, but no one felt much like celebrating or rejoicing. My mother met us at the house that morning to bring Jacob and Jerrod home so we could spend the day together as a family.

Robby and I unloaded the large stroller the hospital had loaned us and some of Justin's personal belongings. We sat Justin in the stroller and wheeled him into the room he had shared with Jacob—all the while talking cheerfully to him, hoping the sight of home would trigger a reaction, but there was nothing. Justin remained silent. His eyes opened but he didn't appear to be looking at or seeing anything in particular. It was more than I could bear to watch him return to his room as just a shell of the child who had so joyfully skipped out of the door just months earlier. I struggled to hold back the tears, but I could no longer speak around the lump in my throat that threatened to choke me. I swallowed hard and tried once more to break the silence, but when I looked down I saw Robby kneeling in front of Justin's chair silently sobbing, his head buried in his hands and his shoulders shaking with emotion.

Reality slammed into me with brute force. I stood frozen with grief as the tears streamed down my cheeks and dripped from my chin. I couldn't comfort my husband. I couldn't change Justin or the situation. I couldn't move. I just stood there and watched helplessly as Robby finally poured out his pent-up grief. When we joined my mother and the boys in the living room, I couldn't help but notice that she, too, had been crying. Again I felt obligated, but helpless, to help those I loved with their grief—I couldn't even handle my own emotions.

After Justin had been moved out of the ICU, grandparents had brought Jacob and Jerrod to see him, but the boys had not wanted to get very close. This changed version of their brother scared them. When prompted to speak to him, they would cautiously say a few words, their high-pitched little voices soft and timid. They spoke to him as they might speak to a new baby or a strange dog. Now that he was home, they were even more timid.

That day passed slowly and awkwardly. No one was very comfortable around Justin, and I found it difficult to care for him at home. I was afraid to lay him flat on the bed because his hospital bed always elevated his head slightly, and I didn't know if he might have some reflux because of the feeding tube. Choking was a major concern. I didn't want him to aspirate and confirm our inability to care for him at home, so I was keenly aware of his positioning while I was changing him. I did discover I could prop him up in a stuffed chair in the living room, and he seemed to be reasonably comfortable—this gave him some relief from sitting in the stroller all day. Neither of the boys wanted to stay in the house with Justin. Even Robby spent part of the afternoon outside, leaving Justin, Jennifer, and me in the house alone. But caring for Jennifer was much easier at home, and I was convinced that I was ready for Justin to return.

On Monday we met once more with Justin's care team, including his doctors and his therapists. Even though I felt confident that it was time for him to go home, no one on the team would recommend his discharge from the hospital—not because they felt it was better for Justin but because they felt his care would be difficult for us. Although Robby supported me, he too had reservations about how much Justin's care would disrupt our family, but he didn't voice them in the meeting. I felt Justin's hospital stay was far more of a disruption to our family. However, I also struggled with another fear: I was afraid if he didn't come home now, he might not ever come home.

Ultimately, the decision was our right to make as his parents, and his care team finally consented to let Justin go home with the agreement that we would bring him back to the hospital five days a week for three hours of therapy a day. We agreed. We knew Justin needed intensive therapy and we knew of no other options. I realized that five trips a week would be difficult and almost as disruptive to our family, but that day it didn't matter: Justin was finally coming home.

⬿ Chapter 12 ⬾

Unprepared Hearts

Lord, you know the hopes of the helpless.
Surely you will hear their cries and comfort them.
Psalm 10:17

Once it was determined that Justin was indeed coming home, plans were set in motion to begin preparing the house for his return. We rearranged our three-bedroom home so Justin could have his own room. Gone were my plans for a pink and purple nursery for my long-awaited baby girl, but I had no regrets. Justin was coming home and my family would soon be reunited. The rehab coordinator contacted a medical equipment company that came and set up a hospital bed and a feeding pump in Justin's new room. We were also connected with a medical supplier who would deliver Justin's incontinence and g-tube supplies.

The medical equipment company that supplied Justin's hospital bed also had a representative who specialized in customizing wheelchairs for handicapped children. He met with Justin's physical and occupational therapists, Robby, and me to customize a wheelchair for Justin. There were many different frame and seating styles from which to choose. We could also customize the color of the frame and the color and material of the seat. When he was done, we had ordered a dark navy blue frame that folded to make it easier to stow in the back of our small car when traveling. It contained a tilt-in-space system that allowed the entire seating system to be tilted backward in a reclining position. This would change pressure points on his body and use gravity to encourage him to rest his head on the headrest rather than pulling it forward to his chest. The dark, mottled navy seat was made from a washable vinyl. It was custom designed to fit his body and had a five-point harness, a wedge to help keep the tone in his legs relaxed, adjustable side supports, and a head support. Armrests were attached to the frame and covered in a soft rubber. The footrest had straps to keep his feet in place and his knees bent—thus relaxing his high tone since Justin had a tendency to stiffen and kick his legs out straight whenever he was upset or startled.

Justin's therapists recommended he have both a stander and a walker at home, so we ordered these as well. In addition to all the equipment already in place or on order, we ordered a large car seat to use in transporting Justin to and from therapy. However, once it came in, we realized it would not fit in our small car, and we could not afford to buy another. Our solution was to transport Justin to and from therapy buckled in the front seat, which reclined enough to keep him comfortable. We soon felt as though we had enough medical equipment to start a small business. One of the most functional items for Justin did not come from the medical equipment company. Dwain and Cammy, Robby's sister and brother-in-law, purchased it for him. It was a small, child-size recliner. When tilted back into a reclining position, it fit and supported Justin perfectly. It became one of the most used pieces of equipment Justin owned—he sat in it several hours a day. Justin seemed more comfortable in the padded recliner than he did in his custom wheelchair.

Two weeks after his birthday trip home and more than fifteen weeks after he entered the hospital, we brought Justin home. That first night I managed to make supper, feed Jennifer, and get Jacob and Jerrod ready for bed before Justin began his nightly routine of intense prolonged crying. I knew from experience in the hospital that it was better to wait until his cries were less intense before starting his feeding pump because he was prone to throw up while he was crying. So when he began to cry, which was no longer silent since the trach valve was inserted, I changed him into his pajamas and raised the head of his bed until he was almost in a sitting position. Then I gently bent his legs at the knees and propped a pillow underneath them. I pulled up both side rails and left him to cry while I conducted our usual bedtime routine with Jacob and Jerrod. As I had done while he was in rehab, I planned to return soon and sing to him until the crying stopped.

Robby was appalled. Since he had returned to work, he had not witnessed many of Justin's crying episodes. As Justin's screams could be heard echoing from every corner of the house, Robby quickly sought me out and asked why I was not trying to console him. I told Robby I would see what I could do, but that while Justin was in rehab, I had not been able to do anything that would really console and quiet him. I had indeed tried many things, but his bed in rehab was very tall—almost like a large crib—and I had not been able to just take him in my lap and try to comfort him, so all of my efforts had been performed from his bedside.

That night while the boys joined their daddy in front of the TV, I put Jennifer in her car seat and carried her into Justin's room, closing the door behind us. Then I pulled Justin into my lap and gently bent his legs until his tone relaxed. I began to rock gently back and forth with one arm wrapped around his shoulders to support his body while using that hand to hold both of his arms down in his lap to prevent him from drawing them toward his chest. I used the other hand to keep his knees bent and my cheek against his forehead to keep his head from pulling down and constricting his trach. I rocked Jennifer's car seat with my foot. Jennifer was a very calm-natured baby, and she rarely cried unless she was hungry. She never seemed disturbed by Justin's cries although most of the adults on the rehab floor were visibly upset by his nightly episodes of neuro-crying. Each night when he began, we were often left unattended from there on out, but Jennifer would sleep even when Justin was crying just a few feet away. While I rocked, Jennifer dozed and Justin's cries slowed and shrank to a whimper.

This was the most success I had ever had in calming Justin during one of these crying episodes, so I sat there and rocked him, my arms aching with fatigue and the muscles in my legs cramping with his weight and the stress of both holding him and rocking Jennifer. I rocked both of them for over two hours before Justin finally began to relax and breathe deeper, slowly drifting off into a light sleep. I lowered the head of his bed slightly so it was still at an incline and continued to rock him until I thought he was sleeping soundly enough to slip him into bed without disturbing him. That accomplished, I attached his feeding tube and set the pump.

Justin was sleeping now, so I gently lifted Jennifer from her car seat and settled myself on the floor to nurse her. By the time I finally opened the door and slipped out of Justin's room, it was long past Jacob and Jerrod's bedtime. Jacob had fallen asleep on the couch while Jerrod was still intently watching TV. I gathered them both up and carried them to bed, where I kissed them and tucked them in without their usual story or prayers. To put them to bed like that made my heart ache. I felt that despite my best plans, I was still unable to care for all of them.

Thus began our nighttime routine. I would shut myself in Justin's room with Jennifer in tow and rock them both until Justin finally went to sleep. Jacob and Jerrod would watch TV or be sent to bed by their daddy without the story time or prayers that had so long dominated their nightly routine. Often they were asleep before Justin was finally settled. My heart longed to hold them in my lap and read to them. I wanted them to be sent off to sleep with prayers and loving caresses, but I alone could tend both my youngest and oldest, and Robby was unfamiliar with tenderly ushering little ones into dreamland.

In just a few days, a routine began to emerge. During the day, Jacob and Jerrod either stayed with Mamma while I took Justin to therapy or I toted them with me as extra hands to help me with their brother and baby sister. When we were all home, I felt absent from them as they entertained themselves, often spending much of the day outside or in their room. They would offer to help with housework and would sometimes help entertain Jennifer when I was busy, but they were still little boys. Jacob had just turned four and Jerrod was not yet three, so they were still timid and frightened by their brother.

After everyone was settled for the night, there was usually supper to put away and clean up. Robby would often urge me to just sit down and watch TV with him, but I could not relax knowing that a mess still awaited me in the kitchen. Most nights Robby was ready to turn in for the night by the time I was done. Many times we would not even get to sleep before Justin was again awake. Though his nighttime crying was rarely as intense as the neuro-crying that occurred before bed, I would still get up and again rock him in my lap until he was quiet. Between Justin and Jennifer, I was usually up four or five times a night. Many times I would sleep on the couch to avoid disturbing Robby—a habit he found irritating. I was never sure if he was frustrated because I was in and out of bed disturbing his sleep or because the only alternative I could find was to sleep elsewhere rather than beside him.

I was beginning to understand that while I had prepared our home for Justin's return and I had prepared myself for his care, his hypersensitivity, and his nightly crying episodes, I hadn't known how to prepare Robby, our marriage, or our little boys. Despite all my preparations and plans, I still felt unable to give each member of my family all the time and attention they needed. I couldn't help them understand and accept the changes, changes I myself could not comprehend or fully accept. I was simply functioning—doing what needed to be done—while clinging to the hope that Justin would soon be better. I wasn't prepared for the ongoing pulling of my heart in so many directions, and I could only hope that the changes in our life were temporary.

⌒ Chapter 13 ⌒

Unseen Scars

He heals the brokenhearted and bandages their wounds.
Psalm 147:3

I knew from the beginning that bringing Justin back to the rehab unit five days a week for therapy would be incredibly hard on our family. We lived forty miles from the hospital. Nana worked, but she wanted to help when she could, and Mamma was more than willing to keep the boys while I took Justin to therapy. When it was her turn, Robby would usually take them to her house to save me a little time and to get a minute with his parents. A few times I tried to leave Jennifer there as well, but it interrupted her nursing schedule, which was difficult on us both—particularly on me since she would take a bottle if it were offered. Sometimes I took the boys with me despite the protests of well-meaning grandparents. Although it was hard on the boys since there was nothing for them to do and they would have to sit or play quietly in a corner, it was actually easier to take them. It saved me time in picking them up after therapy. And though they were only three and four years old, they provided extra hands to carry diaper bags, push the wheelchair, and help with Jennifer.

One morning a few weeks after Justin had returned home, we were making our daily trip to the hospital for therapy when I noticed Justin's eyes blinking strangely. He was in the front passenger seat of our small car with his head turned toward the window. His eyes were blinking so rapidly I thought at first he may be blinking at the sunlight, but as I drove, I continued to look over. Although I had no experience with seizures, I had a growing dread that perhaps this was what I was witnessing.

The eye blinking continued without pause, so when I reached Lubbock, I bypassed therapy and took Justin to the emergency room, where I asked if he could possibly be seen by his neurologist. I was thankful I had agreed to let the boys stay with Mamma, but it was not easy managing both Jennifer's car seat and Justin's wheelchair.

Justin's neurologist soon arrived. He examined Justin for a few minutes, then turned to me and said calmly, "Mrs. Campbell, it was wise of you to bring Justin right in. He does appear to be having seizures, and I am going to order an EEG and admit him for overnight observation. I think we will be able to get them under control with medication, but I want to keep him until he stops seizing."

Justin was soon wheeled into a room where a technician began attaching electrodes to his head with putty. The process of connecting the electrodes actually took longer than the EEG itself, and it was over sooner than I expected. When we were done, Justin was taken to a room on the children's floor. I was thankful they had admitted him into a room so quickly. Justin's neurologist arrived later that afternoon with the results.

"Mrs. Campbell, the EEG has confirmed our suspicions. Justin is indeed having seizures. In fact, he is seizing nonstop. Our first course of action is to get them under control as soon as possible, so I'm ordering seizure medication to be administered by IV. We will keep Justin here until he's no longer seizing. I'll have another EEG run in the morning, but hopefully we'll see results quickly." He continued to explain this new condition. "Considerable research has been done in the field of epilepsy, but there is still much we don't know. Seizures are often caused by scar tissue in the brain. It is obvious that Justin's seizures are a result of his brain damage—sort of a short circuit in the brain. This seizure episode may be a one-time occurrence. Once they are stopped, they may never recur. However, we will want to keep him on seizure medication and under careful observation for several months even if there is no recurrence. But I should tell you that it's also possible that Justin may have to remain on seizure medication for many years—maybe even the rest of his life. Many people who are epileptic live normal happy lives."

"What will happen if the seizures don't stop?" I braved the question with hesitation, but I had to know.

"Well . . . we have to stop this continual seizing, and I think we can with medication. However, there are some mixed opinions in the medical community regarding seizures that are never fully controlled. By that I mean, recurring seizures, not continual seizing. Some believe recurring seizures can cause additional brain damage or short circuits to the brain while others feel that all seizures are a result of existing short-circuited pathways and do not cause further damage—they simply reveal the existence of a short circuit."

After he left, I realized he had not really answered my question.

Although his trach had been removed a week after he returned home, Justin still had a port, so seizure meds were soon being administered by IV and Justin responded quickly to medication. He was discharged the next day after his EEG confirmed that the seizures had stopped, and we were sent home with a prescription for one of the most common and effective seizure medications available. The medication came in a liquid base that could easily be administered through his g-tube, and it appeared to be effective in controlling his seizures.

Two days later Justin broke out in a rash; it was an allergic reaction to the medication. Justin had never been on much medication before he went into the hospital for surgery and had no history of allergies to medications, but while he was in the hospital, he developed an allergy to two different antibiotics so I recognized the symptoms immediately. I called his neurologist's office and informed them that Justin had had an allergic reaction to the medication but that I hadn't noticed any more seizures. I was hopeful that the seizing incident was an isolated event and that perhaps the doctor would be willing to see how Justin might do without medication.

I soon received a return call from Justin's neurologist himself. "Mrs. Campbell, I got your message that Justin has had an allergic reaction to the medication. You also said that you haven't seen any more seizure activity. While this is a good indication that Justin has responded well to medication, it is very possible that his seizures will return if we take him off medication. We certainly don't want a repeat performance of his last seizure episode, so I am calling in a different prescription. I would like you to start Justin on it immediately so hopefully he can get some into his system before all of the previous medication has worn off.

While I hadn't noticed any significant side effects beyond the rash from the first seizure medication, it was soon obvious that the new medication made Justin very sleepy. Although he seemed much more relaxed and no longer stiff from high tone, he was also no longer able to bear weight on his legs, and the movement in his right arm was greatly reduced. His physical therapists noted the obvious change and asked, "What seizure medication did they put him on?

"Klonopin," I replied.

"That explains a lot. Klonopin is a popular seizure medication, but it is also commonly used as a muscle relaxant. I am afraid that as long as he is taking Klonopin, his progress may be slowed considerably."

A second therapist agreed. "Yes, Klonopin will make him limp as a rag doll."

"You really should ask his neurologist if there is something else they can give him. Surely they can find something that won't have such a drastic effect on his muscle tone," they suggested.

I made another call to Justin's neurologist and he prescribed yet another prescription—Depakote. Three days passed with no allergic reactions and his tone returned to normal. It looked as if this medication might work. The only drawback was the medication only came in capsule form. To be administered, the capsules had to be opened and the tiny time-release beads emptied into water and flushed through his g-tube. However, these tiny beads floated and often clogged the g-tube. This was very frustrating as it took a lot of effort to clear the tube, but since Depakote didn't create any noticeable side effects, I was content to deal with it—at least for a while.

In addition to physical therapy, Justin attended speech therapy every day. He had a sweet young speech therapist, Susan Frow, who always tried to encourage me despite the slow progress he was making. She worked diligently to desensitize Justin's mouth and tongue and was very patient despite his protests. She hoped to encourage him to chew and swallow once he could tolerate the feeling of food in his mouth again.

While Susan worked with Justin daily to reach an eventual goal of eating, she also observed early on that Justin would open his eyes wide and appear to listen to music— particularly his favorite songs. Occasionally, the corner of his mouth turned up just slightly as though he might smile in response to a favorite. I preferred he listen to children's Christian music, but it was soon apparent that his favorite country songs still had a stronger appeal. She had also observed him wrinkling his nose and using the muscles in his shoulder and arm to swing the back of his fisted hand to his nose in an obvious attempt to scratch it. This prompted her to begin encouraging him to move his arm and his fisted hand to apply pressure to a sensitive switch that activated a cassette tape player and turned on his favorite music. Although he did not seem to make much progress toward purposely activating the switch, it was encouraging to see his expressions change in response to the music.

Almost a month after Justin's seizure episode, I began to notice a strange pattern that once more filled the pit of my stomach with discouragement and dread. Since he had been home, Justin had developed a strong startle reflex to sudden or unexpected sounds. Although he appeared to focus on objects or faces at times, it was soon apparent that he either did not see well or his brain could not anticipate actions that would result in a sudden sound. Anytime a door closed, someone coughed, a cabinet squeaked, or any other unanticipated sound interrupted the silence or background noise of his environment, he would startle. It was a startle reflex very similar to that of an infant. Justin would jump while his extremities—particularly his legs—extended and stiffened. I noticed that immediately following the startle reflex, his eyes would begin to blink and the fingers on his right hand would twitch. The episode did not last long, but it was a seizure. I had been eagerly hoping that Justin could be weaned off his seizure meds soon, so it was terribly disappointing to realize he was still having seizures despite the medication. I knew this was something I would have to report to his neurologist. Since a startle reflex triggered the seizures, I thought perhaps a specific type of seizure medication or some other treatment could control them.

Once again I found myself waiting for Justin's neurologist to interpret the results of an EEG. I was disappointed with the news.

"Mrs. Campbell," his neurologist pulled up a chair and began, "it appears Justin is having generalized auditory reflex seizures. What this means is that although his seizures are triggered by a startle reflex to unexpected sound, we are unable to determine a single source or starting point to his seizures. Just as we noted on some of his earlier tests, Justin's seizures come from multiple damaged areas of the brain. The scar tissue in his brain is creating a short-circuit effect when his brain tries to quickly process incoming information like sound. Sometimes when we can determine where the short circuit starts, certain risky procedures can be performed in hope of eliminating or bypassing the area, but this isn't an option for Justin. He also appears to be having a few small, unnoticeable, spontaneous or breakthrough seizures as well.

"What are breakthrough seizures?" I asked.

"That just means he is having seizures that 'break through' the barrier we hope to create in his brain with medication. It means that although they may not be noticeable, Justin is still having a few small seizures that are not being completely controlled by the medication in addition to the reflex seizures that you noticed. I think our best option is to continue to work with his seizure medication, perhaps increasing the medication he is currently taking or perhaps adding an additional one. You may also want to experiment with environmental controls to help reduce the instances of auditory reflex seizures."

"Will Justin need to have another EEG done after we increase his medication to see if he is still having breakthrough seizures? And if so, how often will we need to do them?"

"We will need to check his medication level and liver function. If we can increase his Depakote, we'll try that first and repeat the EEG in about a month. After that, unless there is some noticeable change, we'll probably not order another EEG. Often observation can tell us how well a seizure medication is working. Since Justin's seizures are obviously related to his auditory input, environmental controls like noise reducing headphones might be helpful to reduce the chances of Justin startling to unexpected sounds."

This was a complex issue as it was becoming apparent that auditory input was Justin's only real connection to the world around him. We couldn't just put earmuffs on him to stifle all the sounds around him without disconnecting him even more from his environment. To completely control the seizures, he would have to live in total silence. And then there was still the high probability that he would have spontaneous seizures that could occur without auditory stimuli, so eliminating auditory input may not have eliminated the seizures completely even if it were an option.

At his doctor's suggestion, we opted to try slightly increasing Justin's dosage of Depakote. Although it did not eliminate Justin's auditory reflex seizures, it was somewhat successful in preventing other spontaneous seizures from breaking through.

Thus began what would prove to be a long battle with seizures. Though Justin's doctor was careful to explain all the terms he used as fully as he could, there was one term I understood all too well. The word echoed in my mind long after we left his office: *scars*. Although Justin had been home several weeks and the weeks were beginning to roll into months, in my mind everything was still temporary and Justin was still in the process of recovery. But there was something permanent about scars. Scars evoked images of wounds that were healed, not wounds that were still healing.

I could not accept the thought of anything regarding Justin's condition as permanent and I clung to the hope that he would continue to improve. Nevertheless, the word lingered in my mind despite my efforts to dispel it. I wondered if my heart, like Justin's brain, bore multiple scars—scars that would permanently interrupt my hope and my faith—or if they were simply wounds that had not yet healed.

⌒ Chapter 14 ⌒

Losing Hope

"O God my rock," I cry, "Why have you forgotten me?
Why must I wander around in grief, oppressed by my enemies?"
Their taunts break my bones. They scoff,
"Where is this God of yours?"
Psalm 42:9-10

When I was a girl, I fell in love with seasonal changes. I loved warm spring sunshine, fresh flowers, new birth, and new beginnings on the farm. I even loved spring winds that whistled around stuffy school windows and made me want to run with loose hair flying and arms flung wide to embrace the changing season. Then spring would melt into bright summer sunshine and I would fall in love once more as I sat eating tomatoes and cucumbers fresh from the garden with my bare feet dangling in irrigation water while I idly watched homemade boats float down the rows. But my affections were fickle and when autumn arrived with cold, damp days and chill winds that tossed colored leaves and tumbled dried weeds, I embraced the changing season with delight, only to abandon autumn when warm quilts, homemade bread, and hot mugs of chocolate made winter's chill seem warm and friendly.

But that love for the changing seasons, that delight in the simple pleasures of life that had lingered from girlhood into womanhood and motherhood, seemed to have disappeared and I had not even noticed. There had been no joy in summer. In fact, I felt as though summer had passed without me and somehow I had missed it. I had abandoned my garden. At some point Robby had plowed it under so I did not have to witness its disarray, but I barely even noticed. When the last days of summer began to fade, there were no trips to the field to deliver supper and watch in wonder as the sun sank as a golden orb behind combines mowing down yellow stalks of corn. Chill winds blew, flowers faded, and leaves turned without my notice as summer drifted into fall and fall quickly became winter. As the holidays approached, I noticed the chill and dreariness of approaching winter, but I couldn't decide if the chill and dreariness came from within or without.

Justin had continued to make small improvements, but his progress was slow. What had started as a pleasant expression and a slight upward turn of the lips was now a smile when he heard something that he obviously remembered fondly. He was drooling less and swallowing more, which gave hope that we might be able to feed him at some point. As his speech therapist, Susan, and I worked toward this goal and with the consent of his doctor, I began giving Justin bolus feeds (a larger amount given at one time) through his g-tube five times a day as part of the process of weaning him from the continuous feed he received at night. This was similar to eating a large meal. The goal was to eventually feed him three bolus feeds a day. We hoped this would help him remember the sensation of being full and feeling hungry.

Not long after we discovered that his startle reflex evoked seizures, Susan discovered something else about those seizures. One day when another therapist entered the room during one of Justin's therapy sessions and Susan saw that the door was about to close, she touched Justin's arm and said firmly, "Justin, the door is about to close."

At the sound of the latch, Justin opened his eyes a bit wider, but he did not startle—and he did not seize. We soon learned that if we could forewarn Justin verbally, we could avoid startling him and thereby avoid a seizure. Soon even Jacob and Jerrod were saying things like, "Justin, I'm going to shut the cabinet," or "Justin, I need to cough."

Sometimes they would gently touch his arm as they had seen me do when they forewarned him of impending noise. It was the first interaction they had with him that was not initiated by an adult. At first their warnings were timid and quiet, but it soon became a natural response to any noise they thought might startle him. It was not only encouraging that Justin seemed to understand what was being said to him, but it also thrilled my heart to see his brothers once more beginning to talk and interact with Justin.

Despite Justin's progress, I desperately needed a break from the daily therapy sessions. It was becoming increasingly difficult to keep up with the demands of a household and four children while traveling forty miles to and from therapy five days a week. Robby's boss, family, friends, and neighbors had all been compassionate and helpful while Justin was in the hospital, but as weeks became months and seasons passed, life had resumed its normal pace and we felt forgotten by most. The meals that had come in abundance while Justin was in the ICU had long ceased coming, and it had been several months since someone had offered to help clean my house or do my laundry. Nana and Mamma continued to help as much as they could, but Nana worked a full-time job. Mamma did not want to intrude on our lives without an invitation, and I was too prideful to communicate my need for help.

As Thanksgiving approached, Justin's therapists agreed to cut his therapy back to just three days a week beginning the week of Thanksgiving and continuing until after Christmas to help alleviate some of the stress that our current schedule was creating for me and our other children. Although we always ate Thanksgiving dinner with our extended families, each year I took great pleasure in decorating our house and our front porch for fall. I usually prepared a turkey and several of our holiday favorites to enjoy at home over the long weekend. That year there were no special meals and no fall decorations inside or out.

However, Thanksgiving passed with the usual holiday fare shared with family. We ate midday at my parents, surrounded by extended family. Then we shared another holiday meal that evening with Robby's parents and siblings and their families. It was an incredibly long day for both Justin and me. I was afraid the stress of the day would manifest itself in our nightly routine, but surprisingly, Justin fell asleep that night without any more difficulty than usual. It was a real blessing considering my exhausted state.

While the family was together for Thanksgiving, Robby's family scheduled a holiday photo session. The plan was to take a group picture that included his parents, the four children and their four spouses, and nine grandchildren. Considering the number of people involved—including Justin and two infants—the photo session was done fairly quickly. Robby held Justin in his lap for the picture. Although his head was turned, he was surprisingly content so the final picture turned out much better than I anticipated. Justin even appeared to be smiling.

The success of the photo session convinced me to go ahead and try for our annual Christmas picture of the kids. This would be their first picture with their new baby sister. I tried not to think about how changed Justin would be in this picture; instead, I focused on how differently next year's picture would look when Justin had recovered more fully. I asked Robby to help me take the kids to the photo session because, unlike the picture I had made when the boys were very little, I wasn't sure I could manage them by myself. However, I thought a group picture to give to grandparents for Christmas would be a nice surprise. I also wanted some individual pictures of Jennifer. I had managed to get Jennifer's picture made when she was a month old, but she had very few snapshots. She was my little ray of sunshine in a very dark world, and I wanted at least a few pictures of her babyhood. Pictures had always been lots of fun, so I thought with Robby to help it wouldn't be hard to get at least a few good pictures.

The morning of the photo session, I carefully dressed the boys in matching sweaters and black turtlenecks I had purchased for the holidays. I dressed Jennifer in a pretty green and white holiday dress she had been given that matched the boys' outfits. When we got to the photo department in Walmart, we discovered it was difficult to maneuver Justin's wheelchair into the small booth. It took several minutes and some rearranging to get him in front of the camera. Then getting them all arranged for the picture presented more obstacles. Justin kept dropping his head forward on his chest and turning it to the right. We were also having some difficulty figuring out how to get Jennifer in the picture since I didn't trust either of the boys to hold her while they stood on a box. We finally propped her in Justin's lap and gave Jacob charge of making sure she didn't slide out. By putting Jennifer's head under Justin's chin, we managed to keep Justin's head up long enough to snap a couple of shots. It was a trying experience, and I'm sure I was not the only one who was thankful when it was over.

A couple of weeks later, I eagerly went to preview the pictures. I knew there wouldn't be many to choose from, but I was hopeful for at least one good picture. During the photo session, I had been so anxious about Jennifer sliding out of Justin's lap that I hadn't noticed the boys' expressions, so when I picked up the pictures and looked into the sad, timid

faces of my little boys, my heart melted. It took all the emotional restraint I could muster to pay for a small packet and make my way to the car, where I sat for a moment and let the tears fall. No one was smiling—it was a vivid reflection of the impact of Justin's brain injury on the rest of our family.

As I sat there, my heart breaking for my children—especially Jacob and Jerrod—I found myself once more begging God to restore Justin's health. Although I had prayed this same prayer with tears and earnestness before, this time it was not to eliminate my suffering nor even Justin's. This prayer was on behalf of my children. I was praying for God to show his mercy and even his justice. How could it be fair or just for my little boys to endure the hardships Justin's handicaps created for them?

Trying to regain my composure and repair my makeup so I could finish my shopping, I found myself struggling with a growing resentment and anger. Where was God? Didn't he know I was still waiting for him to arrive? Wasn't he aware that I was still clinging to a hope that he would come and heal Justin and thereby rescue us? I was trying to serve him. I was thankful for the things I knew were blessings in my life. I was teaching my children to praise and thank him for all the good things in our lives, so why had he not intervened and prevented this horrible tragedy. And why would he not step in and repair it now? If this was a punishment for my sin, then why were my children suffering? If this was for his glory, then when was God going to step in and heal Justin so we could begin to give him the praise and glory?

All these many months, I had felt numb and hollow and God had seemed distant, but I had continued to hope and trust that he would intervene for us. I had expressed that hope to everyone who came in contact with our lives. I had reasoned that perhaps God was delaying his appearance to build my faith, so I had determined to make myself believe and thereby strengthen my faith. But my heart was hollow and I felt completely void of faith and hope. Was faith a feeling? Was it an emotion or was it something more?

As I sat there, heart poured out and tears dried, I felt utterly alone and abandoned. I was surprised by my anger toward God and at the same time utterly ashamed of it. Overwhelmed with doubt and confusion, I no longer knew what to believe. I had always thought if I lived a good life, if I went to church and read my Bible, if I tried to please God, the Lord would protect us and shield us, but I found that the very foundation of my faith had crumbled and taken with it all peace and contentment.

Even the usual excitement and pleasure I had always found in the holidays seemed to have vanished. Holiday decorating was minimal, and no cards went out. There were no homemade matching pajamas or homemade gifts and very few holiday goodies from the kitchen. I had tried not to bemoan the changes to our holiday traditions and continued to cling to the hope that Justin's condition was still temporary. I told myself and others around me that he would continue to improve and next year would be so much better. But when no one was around and I was left alone to care for Justin and my babies, I felt all joy and happiness had left our family and I was helpless to bring it back into our lives.

Chapter 15

Evidence of Providence

"But he never left them without evidence of himself and his goodness. For instance, he sends you rain and good crops and gives you food and joyful hearts."
Acts 14:17

After years of working at the school as a teacher's aide, my mother was without a job that fall because of budget cutbacks earlier that year. Unable to find other employment, she had taken a job as a sitter in a home for disabled geriatric patients in Lubbock when she was unexpectedly asked if she would be interested in a home healthcare job. The work was difficult and Nana worked forty-eight hour shifts followed by forty-eight hours off. Although the job was exhausting and there was much to be done in her own home, she continued to help me whenever she could. Her new job allowed her to be available during the week to help the boys and Jennifer while I took Justin to therapy—something that would not have been possible had she continued working at the school. But the change in jobs would prove to be a blessing in more ways than one with surprising evidence of God's hand still at work in our lives. Later I would look back and see that God had not abandoned us but had set a plan in motion to restore both Justin and me to our family.

This new job was in a field Nana was not pursuing, and she was not particularly interested in home health. However, it provided much needed income for their family, so she was thankful for the position. Little did we know she would be gaining valuable knowledge that would prove to be greatly beneficial to our family. In fact, it would open the door to a whole new world we knew little about.

At her new job, Nana began to learn more about home health care. The patients under her care were serviced by Total Home Health, a home health care agency that provided them with skilled nursing care and contracted with other agencies to provide therapy and services for the patients at the home. As Nana began to get acquainted with nurses who worked for this agency, she learned that one of them, a nurse named Lisa Dillard, had a severely handicapped daughter. She began to talk to Lisa about Justin. Through Lisa she learned Total Home Health also provided services to children with disabilities and Justin could easily qualify for these services.

Slowly, we began to question the hospital administration's reluctance to release Justin to our care. We didn't understand why they insisted that we continue taking him into the hospital rehab center for therapy five days a week even though they obviously knew about the availability of home healthcare services. It occurred to us that perhaps they were motivated by something other than Justin's best interest and the best interests of our family. As my mother learned more about home health care and the services they provided, she was convinced that Justin would not only qualify for home healthcare services, but he could probably receive his therapy at home as well. We were also beginning to understand that as parents, we had the right to choose Justin's healthcare providers and that it was our prerogative to change providers if we were not happy with the care he was receiving.

All it took was a few phone calls and Total Home Health sent a nurse to our home to evaluate Justin, his needs, and the needs of our family. The nurse was Lisa Dillard, who had opened the door to this new world for us. I liked Lisa from the first moment I met her. She was kind and friendly. She was also a skilled and knowledgeable nurse, but as I watched her with Justin, I was struck with a strange mixture of feelings. She spoke to Justin as though he were a toddler, and Justin seemed to respond by opening his eyes and listening; the corner of his mouth turned up slightly as if he might smile. "Hey there, big guy, let's see how you're doin' today," she said in a sweet, high-pitched voice. "Let's look at your tummy," she continued in the same high-pitched voice while she examined his g-tube. "Oh, I see it! I see your tummy!" she cooed.

Although Justin still had not attempted to speak or communicate, I could tell when he was listening—and he was listening to Lisa. I'm not sure which bothered me more: the fact that she spoke to him as though he had the understanding of a very small child or the fact that he responded as though he were pleased. I still thought of Justin as the eldest of four. Although he was just five years old at the time of his surgery, I usually spoke to him as if he were an adult, so it was difficult for me to listen to someone address him as though he had the understanding of a two-year-old.

I listened with a mixture of admiration and disbelief as Lisa shared her personal experiences. "Let me tell you about my daughter, Jamey. She's just a little older than Justin and has severe cerebral palsy. Jamey seemed to be a normal baby, but shortly after her second set of immunization shots, she began to develop problems. By the time she was a year old, she was severely delayed in her development. Oh, but we're proud of our big girl. She can sit up and she likes to roll and scoot around on the floor. She likes to put things in her mouth, so we have to be careful to keep her hair ties out of reach." She paused to smile and then continued, "But she can feed herself with some assistance. She can sit on her special potty chair and she will use the potty. She still wears pull-ups, but we're working on finding some way for her to communicate her need to use the potty. She has some problems with her vision and wears what we call her 'Miss Beasley' glasses." Lisa smiled again and continued her story of the extra work, heartache, lost hopes and dreams, and the special joy that a severely handicapped child can bring to a family. "Jamey is still non-verbal (this was a term I had never heard before), though she does make some verbalizations—kinda like babies coo before they talk. She is profoundly retarded."

She is profoundly retarded.

I felt as though I had been slapped. It was the first time I had ever heard anyone use the word *retarded* to describe brain-injured children. And the first time I even considered that Justin may not be the same little boy inside or that he might not continue to grow and learn as he had before. It was a word I knew well, but it seemed so harsh to hear a parent use it in reference to her child. For Lisa to say her daughter was profoundly retarded was to admit a reality about her child that I had never even considered regarding mine. Later I would come to love Lisa and realize she was being bravely honest and genuinely wanted to help our family accept the reality of what we may be facing. However, the thought of Justin never regaining more than just the ability to sit up, scoot around the floor, and possibly feed himself with the skills of an infant was more than I was ready to accept. All Justin's doctors, nurses, hospital therapists, and even the hospital administration and staff had encouraged us with stories of children and adults who had made complete or near complete recoveries. Those stories were a lifeline of hope—and I was clinging to them.

Lisa was the first to offer us a look through the lens of reality. It felt as though she were ripping that lifeline of hope from my clenched fists and forcing my eyes to open to another world. I resented even the glimpse. I had once had a glimpse—that precious little girl I'd seen in the hallway at the hospital. The image was forever burned into my memory—a memory I had spent months trying to erase. Lisa's reality could not possibly be mine, and I clung tightly to the hope that Justin's condition was anything but permanent.

Despite Lisa's unspoken comparisons between Justin and her daughter, I was extremely thankful for her help and knowledge in a world I knew so little about. Her presence in our lives could not be viewed as simply coincidence. Although I continued to feel utterly abandoned, I know now that God was still present and orchestrating the circumstances of our lives.

Lisa's knowledge of the services available and the ensuing paper trail required to receive them was invaluable.

While Justin was in the hospital, his cardiologist signed all his orders for therapy services, and the hospital submitted them to Medicaid. We had not seen his cardiologist since Justin left the hospital. She had not asked us to bring him for a follow-up visit and had virtually disappeared, but she was the doctor listed on his Medicaid forms and had signed all the medical requests for the therapy services he was receiving from the hospital. I was afraid of the paperwork that could be involved if we changed services and providers. I had no knowledge of what to do or how to get it changed, but Lisa knew the procedure and helped us navigate the necessary paperwork, including changing doctors on all Justin's orders. She spoke to our family physician, Dr. Linton, who was happy to sign the orders for Justin's therapy and homehealth services. The whole process was much easier than I had imagined, and soon everything was in order. Except for monthly neurology visits, our daily trips to Lubbock were now over. A tremendous burden had just been lifted, and I would be forever grateful.

Lisa soon became a regular in our home. She came to help a few hours each week with Justin's daily care. She taught me valuable skills and gave many tips on how to care for him. She also provided invaluable help with Justin's therapy goals for feeding. With Lisa's help, I soon understood the importance of positioning while feeding and saw how Justin's lack of head control had delayed his progress in this area. Together we worked to find a position that was comfortable for Justin and would give him the head support he needed to swallow without aspirating or choking. Lisa suggested that we try feeding Justin while he was reclined in his child-size recliner rather than in his wheelchair. This position worked better than any other we had tried, and within a few months,

Justin was eating small amounts of pureed baby food. She also suggested we put Justin in pull-ups and have his medical supplier order him a support for the toilet. Although his sensitivity to touch and cold made bathroom time so miserable that I did not follow through with our toilet training for long, the pull-ups were so much better than diapers. I hated the bulkiness and institutional appearance of the diapers. The pull-ups seemed to restore some of the dignity he had lost.

Total Home Health contracted with a pediatric therapy service to supply Justin with the therapy he needed. Georgia Blessey co-owned Pediatric Therapy of Lubbock with Pam Baker, a service they had started just a few years earlier. Georgia was petite, attractive, and obviously athletic. She was pleasant but had a businesslike manner and did not waste time in idle chatter. Our first therapy session with her was much like my first meeting with Lisa. I excitedly showed her how Justin could bear weight and stand with support and how he took a step when prompted to walk. Gently, she told me that while that was good and would be helpful in transferring him, walking—even with the assistance of a walker—would not be a viable goal without head and upper-body control. Her goals for him would be much simpler: head control and weight bearing on his arms.

Georgia's company also provided Justin with occupational therapy and speech therapy. We were both pleased and surprised to discover that Susan Frow, Justin's speech therapist from the hospital, also worked for Georgia and Pam, so with almost no gap in service, Susan continued to work with Justin on his feeding and communication. Although we were not making much progress in the area of communication, Justin was beginning to eat and swallow soft and pureed foods. I was thankful Susan could continue her work with him.

With winter holidays behind us and homehealth services now in place, life began to settle into a daily routine that, although still difficult, was much easier to manage. As I looked back on the fall months and our daily trips to Lubbock, I wondered how we had managed those days. It was as though we had traversed a deep gorge on a rickety bridge and somehow all of us had made the journey without falling. I knew it was nothing short of miraculous, but I still felt as though God had abandoned me. I was forever waiting for his grand appearance in this nightmare.

⁀ Chapter 16 ⁀

New Friends

So encourage each other and build each other up,
just as you are already doing.
1 Thessalonians 5:11

After Justin was released from the hospital, the rehab coordinator contacted our local school district to tell them about Justin's brain injury and let the school know he was receiving therapy services Monday through Friday at the hospital. The school principal then contacted us and told us he had met with the special education diagnostician for the district and the elementary special education teacher. It was their opinion and the opinion of the hospital rehab coordinator that the current services provided by the hospital were sufficient to meet Justin's educational needs but that we should contact them if this arrangement changed.

When we decided to apply for home health care, I wasn't sure if I should contact the school. I knew I did not want to send Justin to school—not only did I feel it would not be in his best interest, but despite the added work and responsibility, I still wanted Justin home. I knew I had the freedom to homeschool my normal children, but I was not sure of the law regarding special needs children.

I vaguely remembered hearing about the Texas Home School Coalition (THSC), an advocacy organization for homeschool families in Texas. Their home office was located in Lubbock, so I looked them up in the phone book and called. They were very helpful and told me I had the same rights to homeschool my special needs child as I had to homeschool my normal children. I didn't think Justin had been enrolled in the local school district when the hospital had contacted them about his therapy, but THSC suggested I make sure the school did not have him listed as enrolled and homebound. They also gave me a phone number for NATHHAN (National Handicapped Homeschoolers Associated Network—now National Challenged Homeschoolers Associated Network).

I gathered up my courage and called the school. I did not know what to expect and was concerned they would not support my decision to keep Justin home. I was quite relieved to learn Justin had never been put on the school roll, so there was no need to withdraw him. The lady I spoke to at the school even informed me that the school could provide therapy for Justin as a homeschooled student if I requested it. I think the school officials were just as relieved that I wanted to keep him home as I was to learn they would not insist he attend.

My next phone call was to NATHHAN. I had many questions, beginning with, "How do you educate a child who can't even talk or communicate?" The woman I spoke to was sweet and compassionate. She listened, offered words of encouragement, and explained a little about Individual Education Plans (IEPs). She also took my contact information and said she would try to put me in touch with another homeschool family with a special needs child in our area.

It was not long before I received a call. The phone jangled several times before I could empty my hands of wet dishes to pick it up.

"Hello, is this Sheila Campbell?" a pleasant voice asked.

"Yes, this is she." I expected the lady on the other end to identify herself as a receptionist from one of Justin's doctors or therapy offices. I was pleasantly surprised when she continued.

"Hi, I'm Janet Norton. I received a call from NATHHAN saying you have a handicapped son you are homeschooling and would like to meet someone else doing that." She paused, waiting for my confirmation.

"Yes!" I blurted out. "Yes, I started homeschooling my oldest son Justin, who is six, last year, but he recently suffered brain damage and now I don't even know where to begin with him."

"Oh, I'm sorry to hear that. It sounds as if we have similar challenges. I have five children I'm homeschooling including Janell, who is my youngest and one of a set of twins. Janell and David are six years old. David is a normal, healthy little boy, but Janell was born with cerebral palsy. The lady from NATHHAN said you have several questions about homeschooling a non-verbal child. Janell is non-verbal. I don't know how helpful it would be, but I would be happy to talk to you about what we do." Janet went on to tell me about Janell. Although we talked more about the strengths and challenges of simply raising handicapped children than we did about schooling them, I was thoroughly enjoying the chance to talk to someone with a similar situation. The Nortons lived in Amarillo, about 100 miles north of us. Janell also suffered from seizures and saw a pediatric neurologist in Lubbock once every three months.

"I would love to meet you and your family," Janet declared as we neared the end of our conversation. "Would you mind if we stopped by for a short visit on our way back from Lubbock in a few weeks?"

I was elated. I wanted to ask her so many questions about homeschooling and caring for a handicapped child. I had made a couple of homeschool friends before Justin had surgery, but we had only met a few times and I had not gotten to know them very well before our world was turned upside down. I had not contacted them since we had come home. One of my best friends had moved out of state while Justin was in the hospital and another nearby girlfriend from high school was simply in a different season in her life. Although I was lonely for the fellowship of women, it was difficult for me to talk to old friends. I didn't know what to say to them, and they didn't know what to say to me. I felt as though they were afraid of me or perhaps afraid of what had happened to my family.

Almost immediately after Justin came home, Robby was ready to return to church. I, on the other hand, was not ready. I was viewing the situation from a practical viewpoint—to get all four children fed and clothed and ready for church was a major undertaking. And there was no place to take Justin; I wasn't sure he would sit quietly through service. I was also angry with God, though I wouldn't have admitted it. I felt as though God was late arriving and I was not ready to worship him until I knew he was there. I was clinging to a hope that he might still intervene and begin to heal Justin. I wanted to wait until those miracles actually began to happen before we began attending church again.

In my mind, Justin's appearance wasn't a testimony to the things God would do but rather a testimony to the things God hadn't done. With all Justin's care, therapy five days a week, a new baby, a two-year-old who was still not completely potty trained, and my four-year-old now shouldering the burden of becoming both my right-hand man and the eldest child, life was too complicated and too hard to be anything but temporary. I felt detached from any emotion—I was merely surviving. Church attendance represented something normal and ordinary and far removed from what I was living.

My withdrawal from church and our church family had left not only me but also our entire family isolated and without friendship, fellowship, and the encouragement we all need from other believers. However, my life had been so focused on caring for my children that I hadn't even noticed how lonely I was for interaction with other women until I got the call from Janet. I desperately needed a friend.

I loved the Norton family from the first moment we met. Don, Janet's husband, carried Janell into the house as though she were an infant and sat with her in his lap as we visited. She was tiny and frail, but she had big eyes that took in everything around her. She was alert and happy and watched the other children with interest. In contrast, Justin sat in his recliner with his eyes closed most of the time and appeared to doze. I knew by his expression that he was listening more than he appeared to be, but his inattention to visitors was discouraging.

I watched as Don and Janet's older daughters talked to Janell and doted on her. They brought her a drink and held a rag under her chin while they offered her a sip. Before they left, the girls offered to change her. They treated her as though she were their infant sister—as though it mattered little to them that she was six. The whole family seemed to accept Janell's handicaps and easily incorporate her needs into the family without much effort. I loved the way they all helped care for her. I knew it couldn't have always been that easy, but they made it seem effortless—both accepting her limitations and meeting her needs.

Later when I mentioned all this to Janet, she shared with me the struggles she had in the early years after Janell was diagnosed with cerebral palsy and how she had grieved over the loss of a normal, healthy, active child.

My heart had grieved that moment in the hospital when I was first exposed to a child with brain damage and my heart had grieved the day we brought Justin home, but most of the time my heart just felt empty. It was difficult for me even to relate to Janet's grief because I was desperately clinging to the hope Justin would get better, and that hope would not allow me to grieve. I wondered again at the cleaning lady's words, "Tears don't mean you've given up on God." But that's not how it felt. Grieving would mean I'd surrendered to loss. I could not surrender—not yet.

⤜ Chapter 17 ⤝

Comfort in an Ancient Story

I lie in the dust; revive me by your word.
Psalm 119:25

Winter passed slowly. Justin continued to have nightly episodes of irritability and neuro-crying. He never slept through the night but would awaken and cry until I gathered him into my lap and rocked him back to sleep. I was thankful he was no longer connected to his feeding pump at night and could handle enough in his bolus feeds to satisfy his nutritional needs. That made comforting him and repositioning him at night much easier. Many times I would get him comforted and back to sleep just as Jennifer awakened for her nightly feeding. Although I was tired, once both of them were again content and asleep, I often sat awake in the dark house. Lit only by the moonlight streaming in through the windows and the glow from the Dearborn space heater, the quiet house felt peaceful and soothing. God still seemed so distant and I struggled with many doubts about my faith. I felt as if my prayers had gone no further than the ceiling for many, many months, but in those dark moments there was a peace about the house I wanted to cling to. It was as though God were there but just out of reach. At times I felt as though I were Jacob, wrestling with the Lord in the dark hours of the night—struggling to hold onto my faith until he blessed me.

I began to use the nightly interruptions to my sleep as an opportunity to once again read my Bible. To avoid disturbing Robby with a light, I had taped a small flashlight halfway up a thick wooden ruler. That way I could hold both the light and my Bible with one hand if I needed to, or I could place my Bible on the floor beside me and use the ruler to hold it open while the flashlight illuminated the words. In this way, I could read while I rocked Justin or fed Jennifer.

I had not read my Bible regularly in many months, but I was drawn to the Word. Whether it was a desperate desire to recapture the peace and security I once had in my relationship with God or a need to do something to somehow earn a blessing, I couldn't determine. I wrestled with my motives for pushing myself to read my Bible when it was so difficult. I wondered if perhaps it was simply a need for a familiar discipline, but then I found myself questioning why I had ever developed the habit. Did I really believe that purposeful discipline would earn me a blessing? And was that the only object or was there something more? Did I desire to know more about my God so I could make sense of these life-changing events? Was I just looking for comfort and an assurance that God was good? Or perhaps there was something else compelling me. Whatever the reason, I still found the words of the psalmist comforting—particularly the psalms in which David also cried out to the Lord asking God how long he must wait for deliverance. I knew there was a happy ending to David's story. God rescued him.

One day in early spring, both Jacob and Jerrod began to run fevers and develop cold symptoms. Somehow we had managed to make it through most of the winter without any illnesses. I was so busy trying to meet the needs of my family that the fact we had gone so long without a cold had escaped me.

That day it became starkly evident how very little attention the boys received from me. I dressed them and fed them, but they spent most of the day entertaining themselves. Story time was now non-existent, and I doubted if Jerrod even remembered ever having story time. There were no walks, no playtime together, and even nighttime prayers had disappeared from their lives. What little time I did spend with them involved teaching them how to help with various household tasks. I relied heavily on their assistance.

But as the cold began to take its toll on his usually cheery demeanor, Jerrod was cranky and soon in tears. I gave him some medicine, taking him in my arms and rocking him for the first time since Justin had come home. Jerrod had been such a cuddly baby. He had always enjoyed lap time, but somehow after Justin's surgery and Jennifer's birth, he had suddenly seemed big and I had two others to hold and rock. Now I was struck by how little he still was—after all, he was barely three. As the cold medicine began to take effect, Jerrod snuggled into my arms and went to sleep. I stood up and gently carried him into his room only to discover that Jacob, also hot with fever, had wrapped himself in a baby blanket and was asleep on his bed. I laid Jerrod down, gently gathered Jacob up in my lap, and began to cry. Out of the depths of my broken heart, I thanked God for the cold the boys had and how it had opened my eyes to how much I was neglecting their needs by putting everything in my life "on hold" while I focused on Justin's recovery. I prayed for strength to meet the needs of all my children and wisdom to know how to care for everyone until Justin was better. It was probably the first time in my life that I really thanked God for a difficult situation, and it was probably the first time I could see the good in the midst of the bad.

I held Jacob in my arms and prayed while silent tears ran unchecked down my cheeks. He stirred and woke up, and his tender heart was touched by my tears. "It's okay, Mama," he said in his little four-year-old voice. "I'm not going to be *very* sick."

I paused and considered his meaning for a moment. With a jolt, I realized why he said those words. No one had really talked to the boys about what had happened to their brother. We didn't understand ourselves what had happened and I never thought about how confused or frightened they may be. I smiled through my tears, blew my nose, and dried my face.

"I know, honey," I said gently. "Mama's just sad that you're sick and had to go to bed by yourself. You won't get sick like Justin. I'll get you some medicine and before long you'll feel a lot better."

Then I picked him up and carried him into the kitchen, sat him on the cabinet as I had when he was a toddler, and got him some medicine and a small cup of coffee with sugar and milk—one of his favorite treats and one he had not had in a long time.

Treating the boys' cold symptoms was not difficult, but as the day passed and evening began to fall, Jennifer also began to suffer from cold symptoms. A stuffy nose made it difficult for her to sleep and I found myself sitting up late into the night rocking her in her car seat while I comforted Justin. Then I carried her on my hip while I tended to the boys. Finally I held her in my lap and rocked her while she dozed. Just before dawn, she settled into a deeper sleep and I set her in her car seat and carried her into the bathroom with me so she would not disturb anyone while I showered and changed clothes. By morning, Justin was also running a fever and displaying cold symptoms. I was thankful Justin had skilled nurses to help me know how to treat his symptoms.

After Justin's nurse assessed him and put in a call to Dr. Linton, the doctor was gracious to call in a prescription for all the kids so I didn't have to bring them into the clinic. Taking all of them anywhere was still difficult. Though to my knowledge Dr. Linton had no personal experience with the difficulties I faced each day, she was compassionate and always willing to help where she could.

The next two days followed the same pattern as the first: I tended to sick children day and night. I never went to bed during those first three days of illness, but by God's grace, I managed to keep going. It was during those three long nights spent holding and comforting sick children that I discovered a comfort of my own in a passage of scripture I had often avoided or passed over quickly as I read through the Bible. I was trying to open my Bible to a passage in Psalms when it opened to the first chapter of Job. I knew the story of Job, but I had never understood the story nor could I relate to Job's loss. I did not *want* to understand or relate. But that night the first few verses caught my attention and the book of Job came alive for me. I read the entire book twice during those long nights. I now had a taste of loss and I could understand its bitterness. I was confused and hurt and wondered if perhaps—as some had suggested—my own sin had caused this awful tragedy. However, I found great comfort in Job 7:20 as I read from my old King James Version, "I have sinned; what shall I do unto thee, O thou preserver of men? . . . And why doest thou not pardon my transgression, and take away mine iniquity?" Although it was a question, it seemed apparent to me that Job wasn't relying on his own righteousness (as I once thought) but on God's ability to pardon transgressions. Job was confident sin had not brought these terrible tragedies on him because he trusted in a God who was able to preserve and forgive sin.

It was also comforting to know that God was not punishing Job. I had stumbled on a reaffirmation for my own faith in a God who was able to forgive and pardon my sin. Overwhelming relief washed over me as I was reminded of 1 John 1:9: "If we confess our sins to him, he is faithful and just to forgive us our sins and to cleanse us from all wickedness." I had sent countless prayers heavenward asking for forgiveness, hoping that some unknown sin was not separating me from God or preventing Justin's healing. Somehow, in these scriptures I became confident that tragedy was not always the result of sin.

As I read the counsel given to Job by his friends and Job's responses, I felt his anguish. I could identify with Job as his friends tried to justify and explain the attacks against him and the horrible tragedies that had befallen him. I had seen and heard fear and uncertainty in the voices of my own friends and family as they tried to explain why God had allowed this to happen or why God had not stepped in and rescued our family. They weren't always as blunt as Job's friends had been, nor was I as uninfluenced as Job. I was given books on how to pray, so I tried to pray harder. I was given scriptures on faith, so I tried to have more faith and felt defeated by my unbelief. We had called on the elders to anoint Justin with oil and pray over him. We had Spirit-filled ministers who believed in miraculous healings pray over Justin. None of these things were bad. I know God could have chosen to heal Justin at any time through any means, but nothing changed. Justin remained severely handicapped.

I still clung to the hope that God would eventually heal Justin, and I could not understand why he hadn't yet. I also knew that behind the advice and gifts were those watching who were just as hurt and confused as I. They needed a formula. They needed God to work or to explain why he hadn't because if he didn't, then they too were vulnerable to pain and suffering. It occurred to me that I was just as guilty of this line of reasoning as they were—that's why I had always avoided the book of Job. I did not want to think the God I served would allow suffering. So I understood why it was easier for some to believe that familial error—some hidden sin or unbelief—had allowed this tragedy and was preventing God from healing Justin than it was to believe God was in control. But as I read the book of Job, I found myself surrendering to the possibility that perhaps there were forces or reasons behind this trial we were suffering that were unknown to me. I was convicted by Job's obedience, his loyalty to God, and his faith in God's omnipotent power.

Though Job knew nothing of Satan's attacks, he knew God was sovereign and in control of the situation. And he remained firm in that belief. Job accepted his loss as coming from God. Almost immediately after learning of the tragedies that had befallen him, he proclaimed in Job 1:21, "The Lord gave me what I had, and the Lord has taken it away. Praise the name of the Lord." As I read Job's story, this verse was strangely comforting and intriguing. There was something in it I could not quite grasp. I found myself coming back to it many times as the years passed.

I also found an odd comfort in God's powerful response to Job, although I was a bit frightened by it. God seemed to be harsh as he pointed out Job's weaknesses and limitations as a human and God's unlimited power. But this began to restore and even build my faith in an omnipotent and sovereign God. Of course, many find the end of Job's story happy because God restored Job's wealth and gave him more children, but as I read though the book during those long nights I was not particularly comforted by God's restoration of Job's wealth. I kept thinking about the children Job lost—children who remained dead.

God still did not seem like a loving father but rather like a stern and silent father who had made a decision I did not understand, but I found some peace and faith in accepting that he was in control. It was not a solid faith—just a tiny little seed of faith still shrouded in a shell of grief and growing anger, but for the first time in almost a year God no longer seemed distant.

☞ Chapter 18 ☜

Abandoned Again

O God, you are my God; I earnestly search for you.
My soul thirsts for you; my whole body longs for you in
this parched and weary land where there is no water.
Psalm 63:1

Slowly, the days passed and spring arrived. With the coming of spring, many events of the past year replayed in my mind. I remembered the little boy who slid down the fireman's pole at Kidsville and tried to swing higher than his friend. A red bicycle and red hair flashed through my memory. Fresh garden soil brought back memories of tomato planting. The first anniversary of Justin's surgery approached, reminding us how much time had passed since that dreadful day. It seemed unbelievable; I felt as though I were walking through a dream and at any time would wake up and the nightmare would be over. But it was a waking dream and seemed to be unending.

Total Home Health continued to provide nursing care and therapy services for Justin. With the help of Lisa and

Susan, Justin was now eating and beginning to drink liquids without choking or aspirating. The process of providing him with enough liquids to stay well hydrated was difficult and required a lot of time and patience, but I was determined to have his feeding tube removed. Finally, after going several weeks without using the tube and at the recommendation of Lisa and Susan, Dr. Linton agreed to remove the feeding tube. I rejoiced as the final tube was removed and Justin was left with only scars to remind us of all the pumps, wires, and tubes his life once depended on. The feeding tube was Justin's last remaining external support. In my mind, removing it would finally complete the first step in the long process of restoring Justin to the child he once was. It was our last connection to those awful days spent in the ICU, and I was ready to put those days far behind us. The only other remaining external support were his incontinent supplies—his pull-ups—but it was my hope that one day those too would disappear. I was certain this accomplishment would open the door to a new phase in which his improvement would begin to accelerate.

As the days got warmer, I longed to go outside and enjoy the fresh air and sunshine with my children, but it was difficult to take Justin out for very long because I had no place for him to sit. In the house, he went back and forth from his small child-sized recliner to a large overstuffed recliner we had purchased with Robby's Christmas bonus. Although his wheelchair had a tray and was able to tilt and recline, it had no support for his arms in the reclining position. Justin would fuss and cry while in his chair, so I rarely used it. It stayed in his room until we needed it for transporting him somewhere. Justin did spend some time in his stander each day, but it was impossible to use it outside. I would lean the stander back against his bed or a large chair in the living room and position Justin in it, adjusting all the supports that held him upright in a weight-bearing position on his feet. He usually fussed and cried the entire time he was in the stander. His therapists told us that bearing weight was painful on muscles that had atrophied and must be rebuilt. But I endured his cries because I wanted his muscles to be prepared to function when his mind was once again able to control them.

At Georgia's recommendation, we had taken Justin to a pediatric orthopedic clinic in Lubbock, where they did another series of serial casting on his feet and outfitted him with ankle foot orthotics (AFOs) that fit into high-topped tennis shoes. These replaced the shoes with the metal brace the hospital orthopedic specialist had designed for him. I liked the AFOs much better—the hard plastic braces supported his feet well. Although they required that each foot be stretched until the muscles relaxed and gave in to the straightened position, once they were on, they seemed to help considerably with the high tone in his legs. I quickly learned how to stretch each foot until it relaxed into the correct position and then to slip it into the plastic brace and attach the Velcro straps holding it in place. I then slipped his foot—brace and all—into his tennis shoes. When I bought the new tennis shoes to accommodate his AFOs, I remembered the new shoes he had received for this fifth birthday and his funny comment that he didn't need new shoes because he didn't wear shoes—he preferred to just go barefoot. Somehow I knew he would probably never again run barefoot over soft summer grass, and the thought was almost unbearable. It made the mundane task of buying shoes an emotional ordeal.

The walker that was ordered for Justin when we left

the hospital, a large contraption much like a gigantic baby walker, had been parked in a corner of his room for most of the winter. It was big and bulky and took up a lot of space in our small house. His new physical therapist, Georgia Blessey, felt standing in his stander was just as beneficial, though she did not discourage us from using his walker because it did encourage him to develop some control over his gross motor skills. Now that the days were warmer, the walker found a place outside. Every afternoon after the morning work was done and afternoon naps were finished, I took Justin and Jennifer outside in the shaded front yard. I put Justin in his walker and Jennifer in a playpen to keep my now curious little crawler out of mischief while I worked with Justin to encourage him to move the walker forward on his own. He could not maneuver the walker at all, but could make it creep forward a few inches at a time as he attempted to walk with his right foot. His left foot would move, but he could not manage to pick it up and actually step. Each time he stepped with the right foot, I would wait until I saw movement in his left foot and then help him pick it up and take a step. In this way, we managed to creep slowly across the front yard while Jennifer entertained herself in the playpen. It was not relaxing time spent just enjoying the day, but it did get us outside for a little while.

Jacob and Jerrod would occasionally come and view our progress, but they spent most of their time playing in the tree house their daddy built for them or playing in the backyard on the swing set or in the sandbox. I desperately missed those summer days when I took the boys on walks down the turn rows and into the fields to watch irrigation water run and float homemade boats made of sticks and anything else that would float. I remembered how we had spent our time observing bugs and rocks and just enjoying the afternoon together, and I was afraid the boys no longer remembered those days. I wondered if I would ever again be able to spend moments just enjoying life with all my children. I felt as though Jacob and Jerrod were left to discover the great wonders and simple pleasures of life on their own, and I feared I would never again be able to share those discoveries with them. They seemed happy and content. I was glad they had each other, but I desperately missed them although I spent every day with them.

While Justin was in the hospital, our hometown had set up a trust fund for him at the bank. Robby decided to take some of the money donated for Justin and use it to build a wooden deck with a ramp over the concrete step on the back porch. He also purchased some castor wheels and mounted them to Justin's little recliner. This child-sized recliner accommodated Justin's sitting needs well and put him level with the boys while they played. We also used it as a feeding chair and hoped it made Justin feel as though he were a part of everything going on around him. With the new deck, we could roll Justin out on the back porch and let him sit in the shade of a large umbrella while Jacob and Jerrod and even Jennifer played in the back yard. Although observing their play was better than not being with them at all, I still felt as though Justin and I were on the outside looking in at a world we could not touch or enjoy.

The spring days continued to grow longer. On Mother's Day, Jennifer took her first steps. With those steps, she moved far beyond her oldest brother's skill level. While she was learning to sit and crawl, I had hoped that Justin's progress would keep pace with hers as she learned and he relearned, but the moment she began walking, something inside me almost broke. Maybe my feelings were more intense because it was the anniversary of that tragic day when Justin had slipped into a coma a year earlier. I suddenly felt as though I had missed Jennifer's babyhood while I was putting life on hold waiting for Justin to get better. Now as I watched my baby daughter taking her first steps, I realized the only thing on hold was the everyday joy I once had in just living life and watching my children grow.

Summer passed and we celebrated Jennifer's first birthday, followed closely by Justin's seventh birthday. As his birthday approached, I thought of the toys still in the top of his closet. Last year's presents remained beyond his ability to pick up or even grasp. Although I still clung to a hope that someday he would recover enough to once more play with his trucks, tractors, and Legos, I decided not to purchase anything he could not enjoy right now. His presents consisted of audio books and music cassettes we could play in his cassette player.

Justin was still easily irritated and music could calm him quicker than anything else. Although he did not smile much, the sound of his favorite stories, music, and movies—particularly those that were favorites before he entered the hospital—could bring a look of pleasure to his face and an occasionally a smile or even a squeal of delight, so it was my hope that he would enjoy new stories and songs. I hoped providing him with some little pleasure would make his birthday more bearable for all of us.

And so Justin's birthday passed uneventfully. The memory of his sixth birthday and his first visit home seemed to hang heavy in the air around us and put a damper on the spirit of the occasion, but an audio story of Big Bird brought a smile to his face and, as I had hoped, made the day more bearable. I made a chocolate cake and offered him a few bites, which he ate. However, he rarely ate more than a taste of anything that was not smooth in texture, and the cake was no exception, but his brothers enjoyed it.

Jacob's birthday was only four days after Justin's. Since we felt his birthday had been somewhat overlooked the previous year, we decided to take Jacob and Jerrod to a water park in Plainview for his birthday. Robby's sister, Cammy, and her husband, Dwain, joined us, and we left Justin and Jennifer in the care of Lisa Dillard and Mamma. I was excited to spend some quality time with Jacob and Jerrod, but once we were at the water park I found I could not stop thinking about Justin and hoping that Mamma would be able to handle him after Lisa left.

"Mama, watch me when I come down!" I could hear Jerrod calling for my attention as he hurried back up the walk with his Uncle Dwain to begin the long climb to the top of the water slide. I turned from him just in time to see Robby splash into the pool at the end of the water slide and turn to catch Jacob as he came out behind his dad. In my mind, I could see a seven-year-old redheaded little boy cascading down the slide behind his brother and my heart ached because he was missing from our excursion.

"Did you see Jacob's face when he hit the water?"

Cammy's question interrupted my daydreams and I made an effort to respond with a smile. "Yes, I think he was trying to hold his breath in case he went under. I think he's having fun."

"Yeah, they're having a blast! We'll see if they want to get something to drink when they get back down," Cammy said.

I was surprised at how easily everyone seemed to forget about Justin and just enjoy the day. I tried not to think about him and have fun spending time with the boys, but my thoughts kept drifting back to Justin, wondering how he was doing. I felt guilty putting the strain of his constant care on someone else even for a few hours.

Once more, I felt myself battling against growing resentment and anger, which put a damper on my ability to enjoy the time I had with Jacob and Jerrod. I felt Justin's handicaps were causing the rest of us to miss out on life. I resented being unable to do things together as a family—I wanted us to have fun together. My anger was fueled by a growing fear that we might not ever again do something fun as a family.

The rest of the day passed in a haze. I retained a few mental snapshots of the boys squealing with glee as they zipped down slides and splashed into the pool, but overall I struggled to focus and be present. I was strangely glad to return home to the familiar burden of caring for all four of my little ones.

As anger and resentment grew in my heart, I found myself bouncing back and forth between outrage and guilt. The momentary comfort I had found in the book of Job and the peace I had found in the knowledge of God's sovereignty had somehow disappeared, and I could not recapture them. I tried rereading the book of Job, but to no avail. My best efforts couldn't carry me beyond the first chapter. I went back to reading the Psalms, but my nightly Bible reading seemed once again dry and empty. I often gave up after only a few verses.

My efforts at spiritual discipline seemed futile. Despite my best attempts, I was unable to restore my peace. My spiritual life was an ongoing inward struggle that threatened the very core of my faith. I felt as though I were on a wearisome merry-go-round: up and down, around and around in an "on again, off again" relationship with God. I traveled once more around my concentric circles, slightly more removed from the center of what started it all but struggling with the same emotions and doubts. I felt as though God had stepped down briefly to assure me of his sovereignty and then once again stepped out of my life. My heart was bitter toward a God who seemed like a stern taskmaster requiring more of me than I felt I was able to give as I desperately tried to live a life in obedience to him and be the loving wife and mother I felt commanded to be. My heart was riding a spiritual rollercoaster of a faith that was closely entwined with my emotions. Was faith a feeling or was faith lived out in actions of love even when the heart is broken and the only feelings are pain? I couldn't decide.

I tried to push the thoughts aside, but I was beginning to resent that life was still on hold. I was ready to move on and live and enjoy my children once more, but I didn't know how. I could not understand why the Lord had left me—why he had left us in our suffering. I was angry with God for not showing up and restoring the one thing in which I found complete happiness: my family.

☞ Chapter 19 ☜

Breaking Ground

I will never forget this awful time, as I grieve over my loss.
Yet I still dare to hope when I remember this: The faithful love
of the Lord never ends! His mercies never cease. Great is his
faithfulness; his mercies begin afresh each morning.
Lamentations 3:20-23

During the summer as Jacob's fifth birthday approached, I had wrestled with whether I should send him to school. I had also wrestled with guilt over how little time I spent with Jacob and Jerrod. A year had passed and, although I resented it, in many ways I was still trying to put life on hold in hopes that Justin would get better. I now had a more reasonable definition of *better*: I hoped the amount of time I spent doing therapy with him would lessen as he regained the skills necessary to do something—anything—independently without constant assistance and prodding. Even Jennifer was now able to entertain herself and play unassisted.

Justin dozed intermittently throughout the day, but there

was still no pattern to his sleep-wake cycle, and I suspected that he spent most of the night in and out of sleep. Whenever I wasn't stimulating him, he just sat dozing. Most of the time he was unresponsive to the world around him.

I discovered soon after Justin came home that I could not spend *every moment* of the day tending to his needs. This didn't keep me from trying though. Now as birthdays and anniversaries marked the passing of time, I was beginning to resent how much life we were all missing. Still, I was not sure how to take my finger off the pause button and restart our lives. As I wrestled with thoughts about sending Jacob to school, I realized how desperately I wanted to spend time with him. I could not bear the thought of him spending his day away from the rest of the family. I felt just as I had about Justin two years earlier—perhaps stronger considering how little quality time I was spending with Jacob. I remembered that most of Justin's kindergarten work had been accomplished while Jacob and Jerrod napped and decided I wanted to try homeschooling again. Jacob had a late summer birthday, so if it proved impossible, I could always hold him back and enroll him in kindergarten the next year.

As the cooler days of autumn approached and Jacob's kindergarten curriculum arrived, I found myself continually battling the anger, frustration, and resentment growing in my heart as I tried to find a balance between Justin's care and the needs of my other children, which now included homeschooling Jacob. This battle was incredibly challenging because of the guilt I felt allowing Justin to sit idle while I tended to the needs of my household. This guilt reared its ugly head whenever I devoted any amount of quality time to Jacob and Jerrod doing something Justin could not participate in. I could justify allowing him to listen to audio books or movies while I tended to the others for a short time, but I disliked leaving him like that for very long. I had always limited my children's time with TV and other passive entertainment and encouraged them instead to play creatively. Because I knew Jacob and Jerrod could do so much to entertain themselves with educational games and activities, while Justin could do nothing on his own, I was tempted to relieve the conflict in my heart and just devote most of my day to Justin. Besides, I felt that every minute I could work with him would speed his healing. However, now that school had started, I knew I must somehow make time for Jacob too. This commitment provided me a modicum of relief from the guilt that drove me to try to supply Justin with a full day of activity.

I knew from my experience with Justin that a Christian kindergarten curriculum would have references to God and his creation woven into the daily lessons, so I ordered the same for Jacob. At the time I knew nothing about worldview, but I loved the way the curriculum incorporated a biblical lesson into every academic lesson. This was something I had never been exposed to in my public school experience. Somehow, in my mind I had separated academics from scripture and religion, but when my children were toddlers, I had read them Bible stories and used every opportunity—particularly nature walks and playtime—to teach them about God just as my mother had done for me. After Justin's surgery, nature walks, story time, and playtime had disappeared—along with all talk of God and his goodness. My own struggle to make sense of things had silenced me. How could I tell my children about a good and loving God when he had allowed such an awful thing to happen to their brother?

Now as Jacob and I sat and worked our way through his kindergarten lessons, those simple Bible stories and lessons I had once loved found their way into our conversations again. At first, the stories seemed routine and hollow as I read them verbatim to Jacob without any personal references or discussion. Justin had been naturally inquisitive and his questions had led to some lively discussions, but Jacob was quiet and a natural introvert, so he just listened. Although at times he appeared to be deep in thought, he never voiced his questions. However, gradually, the stories, scriptures, and biblical references in Jacob's daily lessons began to touch something deep within *my* heart. They cracked open a door of hurt that I had somehow managed to close. Many times as we reviewed Jacob's lessons, I found myself swallowing hard in an attempt to eliminate the lump in my throat. Or I would excuse myself to go check on Jerrod and Jennifer in an effort to hold back the tears that threatened to spill. Most of the time I didn't even understand why I suddenly felt like crying, nor could I articulate or locate the source of hurt within my heart. I just knew that something within those stories awoke a longing for God and a longing to believe once more with a childlike faith that he is good.

I was still waiting for God to come in and rescue me from my suffering and heartache. I was still waiting for the freedom to once again enjoy my children. I was still waiting for Justin to be whole—or at least partially restored. I was still waiting for joy to come back into my life. I was still waiting for God to be good.

I had come to accept the fact that Justin may not ever fully recover, but at the same time, I found myself bargaining with God for something better and more complete than what we had. I thought if Justin could talk or communicate, feed himself, and be continent, then I would be happy and life would be easier. I prayed for a glimpse of the future. Something I could hope for and work toward. I tried to imagine what life would look like if Justin were only better. I thought that perhaps if I could keep that image in my mind, I could make it through the days that lay ahead—at least through tomorrow.

But as the writer of Proverbs so wisely stated, "Hope that is put off makes the heart sick" (Proverbs 13:12). As reality began to stare me in the face, my hope was quickly fading and with it all the joy in living that I once had. I did not see that this joy was rooted in my relationship with my children and that through these trials my fingers were slowly being pried from that artificial foundation. This slow prying loose was creating the deep ache in my heart. As my hopes for a better future began to disappear, anger and frustration were being unearthed and my foundation for joy was being broken. The garden of my heart had been plowed deep, and the weeds that usually lay hidden beneath fruitful plants were being revealed. However, the Lord was gentle in this process of stripping away. In his mercy, he provided relief in an unexpected set of circumstances.

⌾ Chapter 20 ⌾

Unexpected Relief

---

*How kind the Lord is! How good he is! So merciful,
this God of ours!... Let my soul be at rest again,
for the Lord has been good to me.*
Psalm 116: 5, 7

I was having such a difficult time dealing with my emotions, I failed to notice that Robby was fighting his own battle with grief, and it was becoming evident in his job. More than a year had passed. By this time, most people—including Robby's employer—thought we should be adjusted to Justin's care and past grieving; in reality, the initial shock was just beginning to wear off. Although we both wanted to close our eyes to the evidence and cling to the hope that Justin would improve, the truth of what we had actually lost was just beginning to dawn on us. The little boy we once had was gone, forever.

We were also isolated and alone. We no longer even talked of attending church. Friends and family with whom we fellowshipped before were few in number. Now that Justin's care in addition to our other three little ones—particularly in the evening—was so intense and difficult, it was almost impossible to maintain relationships.

In December 1994, Robby lost his job. In his providence, God provided another one almost immediately. A change in jobs meant a change in location since Robby worked as a hired hand, and a house on the farm was usually provided with the position. We spent that second Christmas after Justin's surgery surrounded by boxes as we prepared to move.

When we went to look at the farmhouse his new employer, a former classmate of ours, was providing with the job, I could not hold back the tears. It was run down and dirty and smelled of mice. The yard was non-existent. I remembered how much work it had been to dig up sprigs of grass from the ditches and around the irrigation wells and carefully plant them in the yard where we currently lived. It had taken a long time to plant the entire yard. It had taken several years of hard work and tender care for the grass to grow and spread, but now it was thick and lush. Looking at the hard-packed dirt on either side of the front sidewalk, I knew I would have to start over again and wondered if I would have the time or the energy to put in a new yard.

Paul, our new employer, sensed my disappointment.

"It's a little run down" he said, "but I plan to do some repairs."

"We appreciate that," Robby told him. "Of course, we intend to help with the work."

As we walked through the house, Paul talked of the repairs he would make. "I think the best thing to do is replace everything in the bathroom. I think we can probably get some new carpet for the living room and bedrooms and new linoleum for the kitchen and dining area without too much expense."

Robby joined in, trying to raise my spirits. "Some soap and water and a little new paint will go a long way, and it will look better in no time."

I was grateful for Paul's compassion and his desire to provide us with a nice place; however, it did create a problem—we wouldn't have a place to live while repairs were being made on the house. After we discussed our dilemma with our parents, my parents offered to let us to move in with them. With my younger brother in college, they had three extra rooms and a bathroom separate from the primary living area, so we would have our own wing of the house. I was afraid the noise and chaos that was just part of our daily life with Justin's care and three small children would disrupt my parents' routine, but there wasn't another alternative.

Although it had been over eighteen months since Justin's brain injury, his nightly episodes of neuro-crying had not improved. I had mentioned them to his neurologist, but he had been reluctant to prescribe anything to help him sleep because Justin always appeared to be drowsy and dozed on and off during our visits to his office. The neurologist did not want to give Justin anything that would make him sleepier or risk having him slip back into a coma. I think it was difficult for Justin's doctor to comprehend what I was dealing with on a nightly basis because what he observed during our visits was so contradictory to what I described. So I continued to spend many long hours at night trying to keep Justin comfortable and quiet.

"I thought you might like some company," my mother

whispered as she slipped into the bedroom where Justin slept. It was 12:15 a.m., and we had moved into my parents' house just three days before.

"I brought you some coffee with creamer. I thought it may help you relax after he goes to sleep. It's decaf. That's what I drink before bed. It helps warm me up on these cold January nights."

We had replaced Justin's hospital bed with a waterbed a few months earlier. It seemed to help him relax a little better, so it was ideal that one of my parents' extra bedrooms had a waterbed. I eased Justin into the bed and positioned a pillow under his bent knees. Then I began to gently push down on the bed, creating a gentle rocking motion. Justin whimpered, but he didn't resume his crying.

"Thanks." I said, reaching for the coffee.

"Do you do this every night?" my mother asked.

"Yes, he usually goes to sleep before midnight though," I whispered back as I continued to rock and carefully sip the coffee.

After that, she would often join me and stay by Justin's bedside until he went to sleep. I think it was difficult for her to go to sleep knowing I was still awake and trying to get Justin settled for the night. Nana also began helping me feed Justin, and she learned how to give him enough to drink so he was well hydrated. Although it was difficult for me to surrender his care to her, it was so helpful to have someone else who could feed him well enough to administer his meds in his food and give him his allotted liquids. Later, my mother admitted she had not realized how difficult and taxing his care still was, and she was thankful she was given the opportunity to witness it and learn how to help. She clung to the hope even tighter than I did that Justin would fully recover. After witnessing the difficulty of his daily care, she made a secret vow that she divulged many years later to help care for him until he was better.

One night while we were living with my parents, Justin was particularly irritable. I rocked him for several hours and finally convinced my mother to go to bed since she had the responsibility of work the next day. This was not the first time I had passed a sleepless night, but I was concerned that Justin's cries would awaken my parents, so around 2:00 a.m. I finally got dressed, loaded him into our car, and took him to the emergency room in Hale Center.

I was so relieved to find that Dr. Linton was on call. While I rocked Justin on my lap and kept his legs bent to prevent him from posturing, I talked above his cries. I explained that Justin was often irritable throughout the night, but since we were currently living with my parents, I felt he really needed something that would help him sleep. I told her I didn't know what else to do except bring him in and see if they could give him anything to help him relax. Dr. Linton gave him a dose of chloral hydrate, a mild sedative used to treat insomnia. Since it had been more than eighteen months since his brain injury, she felt there was no longer any danger of the sedative sending him back into a coma. She was surprised that his neurologist had not prescribed something to help with Justin's irritability and insomnia. She also gave me a prescription so we could keep it on hand and use it PRN, a Latin medical term that means "to be given as needed." Having this medication on hand became a major turning point for Justin and the rest of our household.

I returned and slipped into the house carrying Justin, who

was sound asleep and limp. I gently laid him on the bed and he slept soundly the rest of the night. The following morning he was very sleepy, but he was also relaxed and less irritable.

I found myself thanking the Lord for the loss of Robby's job and the move into my parent's home, a move I initially viewed as just another bad turn of events in our lives—lives I thought God had abandoned. I could see that God had used those circumstances for good. Without the move, my mother may have never witnessed our daily routine and come to our aid, nor would I have taken the initiative to take Justin into the emergency room during one of his crying episodes and receive the help and medication we so desperately needed. I was beginning to see God was still good. Though I still could not see it in all things, I could see that he was working good in some things that did not appear to be good at first glance. However, I was still not convinced that *all* things work together for good as the scripture, and often my mother, touted.

⌒ Chapter 21 ⌒

Uncontrolled Anger

And so, Lord, where do I put my hope? My only hope is in you.
Rescue me from my rebellion.
Psalm 39:7-8

Soon the farmhouse was ready, and we could move into our new home. Paul and Robby had completely gutted the bathroom and refurnished it with new fixtures. New carpet and flooring had been laid throughout the house and everything had been repainted. It all looked fresh and clean.

There were three bedrooms but one was very small, so we decided to put all three boys in the master bedroom and Jennifer's little toddler bed in the smallest room. Robby and I took the remaining room. Since Dr. Linton had given us a prescription for the chloral hydrate, I had been giving Justin a dose two or three times a week. Even with the sedative, Justin did not sleep through the night and would awaken once or twice to be repositioned, but the episodes of nightly crying had been greatly reduced—enough that we hoped he would not disturb the boys. I was also hopeful that by sharing a room with his brothers, Justin might be stimulated by their conversation and play and encouraged to interact with them.

Once we were established in our new home, life settled into a routine of mealtimes and feeding Justin, therapy, household chores, and school. I was slowly coming to accept that there would be times throughout the day that Justin would have to be left to himself to either doze or listen to an audio book or movie, and—out of necessity—I adjusted the routine I had attempted to establish in the fall to allow more time for Jacob's studies.

Justin still received therapy from the school. They provided two sessions of PT and one session each of OT and speech every week. Justin's therapists were kind and friendly and liked by all my children, so although his sessions relieved me from the duty of daily therapy, they were disruptive to our school day. Everyone else wanted to sit and visit and sometimes even participate in Justin's therapy sessions. Still, relying on the professional therapy sessions helped relieve me from the guilt I felt by not providing Justin with a more rigid therapy schedule myself. Following an established therapy routine also helped relieve some stress as it allowed me more time for everyone else.

However, I desperately struggled with outbursts of anger—usually directed toward Justin when his irritability disrupted our tight routine. He would start whimpering and I would try repositioning him. I would check to see if he needed to be changed. I would offer him a drink. But sometimes I couldn't determine the cause of his discomfort, and his whimpering escalated into uncontrollable screams with his body stiffening and shaking. I would lash out at him with a sharp tongue in a voice I never used with my other children. Instead of pouring out compassion and love on my son who could not communicate his needs, I looked at him as though he were a stranger. There were times I silently wondered if I even loved him. The little boy I once knew had been replaced by a child I could not communicate with or control. I felt that if he would only try to communicate, perhaps I could help him. Surely he knew, I thought—surely he remembered from the training he had received as a toddler that screaming was not the answer and did not accomplish anything.

I felt as if I was starting all over with a new baby, but this baby was big and I could not just pick him up to comfort him or carry him around while I tended to other things. To hold and rock him was an act that required every flexible limb and ounce of physical strength I possessed. It meant completely stopping everything else and focusing one hundred percent of my attention on Justin. I resented the disruption to my schedule that was already full from early morning until late at night with his care. I felt it was unfair to me and to the others who depended on me.

The patience I had that first year was quickly disappearing, perhaps because during that first year I imagined it was all temporary and I could allow myself to put off many routine tasks without worry. That first year my hope for a better tomorrow gave me the strength to tolerate many things for a short time. It's also possible that the hormones my body produced while nursing Jennifer had given me an extra measure of patience. Very likely it was a combination of both, but whatever the logical explanation, the extra measure of patience, strength, and endurance the Lord in his divine providence had granted me during that first year was now gone. I was sleep deprived and drained. I was no longer able to control my own emotions—something I had always prided myself on. I never considered that the control and the inner strength I thought I possessed were not my own but evidence of God's hand in my life. Even the timing of Jennifer's birth and the subsequent hormone boost was evidence of his provision for those days of trial and sorrow. Now those gifts were being stripped away to reveal their true source.

Sometimes as Justin's crying escalated, I would scream, "Shut up!" as I stomped out of the house in a fit of uncontrollable frustration, slamming the door behind me and kicking the porch or slapping the side of the house in my rage. Then I would sit on the porch and wrestle with tears of anger and helplessness until I could swallow them and breathe steadily once more. All the while, my other children looked on in silent shock and fear. Once I had regained some control, I would walk back into the house, gather Justin up, and begin to rock and bend stiffened legs and work to gently relax his arms that were pulled up tight to his chest. I would speak to him softly. "Justin, Mama's so sorry she lost her temper. Mama loves you." This usually brought on a fresh surge of tears—this time tears of guilt and grief until I could once again stop the flow. It seemed I kept a steady diet of swallowed lumps and unshed tears. When Justin finally relaxed and his cries lessened, I would get the attention of my other children and beg their forgiveness.

"Mama is so sorry she yelled at Justin. 'Shut up' is such an ugly thing to say. I don't like to yell at him and say ugly things. It makes me sad."

"That's okay, Mama. We don't want you to yell at Justin

either," Jacob would say as Jerrod gently patted my shoulder. "It makes us sad too."

"It probably makes Justin sad too," I added. "I wish Justin could tell me where he hurts so I could help him, but even if he can't tell me, Mama needs to be more patient with Justin and remember that he probably feels bad and needs Mama to just love him."

"I love Justin," Jerrod would remind me. Their tender little hearts were quick to forgive as they all climbed into my lap and warmly returned my hugs and affection, but my confessions and apologies did little to ease my guilty conscience.

During these episodes, Jacob and Jerrod (now five and four) were both good about watching over Jennifer, who was almost two. Jerrod usually played with her and entertained her in the mornings while I worked with Jacob on his lessons, so it was easy for him to resume their play if Justin's cries and my temper fits disrupted our normal schedule and routine. Although none of them appeared to be very disturbed by my temper, I knew it scared them and was far more harmful to their tender hearts than Justin's disruptive screams. But try as I might, I felt helpless to control my own emotions.

⌘ Chapter 22 ⌘

Desires that Heal

The heartfelt counsel of a friend is as sweet as perfume and incense.
Proverbs 27:9

No one had said much about our decision to keep Justin and Jacob home for their kindergarten years. Both of the boys had August birthdays and could easily be held back if necessary. But as the school year began to draw to a close and I looked into ordering first grade curriculum without any thought of enrolling Jacob in school, several well-meaning family members questioned our choice. "Are you sure it's legal to keep them home?" "How will they ever make friends or learn how to interact with other kids?" "Aren't you worried they won't develop proper social skills?" These were just a few of the questions we received.

I was not surprised there was some concern regarding the legality of homeschooling since it was a topic that had been in the news as the Leeper vs. Arlington case was making its way to the Texas Supreme Court. But I had not put much thought into social skills or the need for my children to have friends—they had one another. Although I wasn't bold enough to ask, I wondered what was meant by "proper social skills." After all, I wasn't planning to keep them locked in a closet nor did they act as though they were raised in a barn. Jacob, who had been terribly introverted and bashful even around extended family before Justin's surgery, had come out of his shell since he no longer had a big brother to talk for him. He was now the big brother for both Jerrod and Jennifer. I was confident that home schooling was the right decision for our family, but I thought I needed help and encouragement to argue and justify my position—I needed some homeschool friends.

One of my closest friends, Sylvia Martin, had moved out of state while Justin was in the hospital, but before she moved, she had introduced me to Michelle Cross. Michelle was a homeschool mom who had two boys only a few years older than mine. I had not spoken to Michelle in almost two years and wondered if she even remembered me, but I had so many questions about curriculum and teaching methods. Homeschooling was still a fairly new concept and Justin's therapists and caregivers often had questions for which I had no answers. Although no one seemed too concerned that I was keeping Justin home and all agreed that a school environment would be difficult for him, especially with his auditory-triggered seizures, there were some concerns expressed by therapists that perhaps we should be preparing to enroll Jacob now that he was approaching six.

In addition to answers that would justify my decisions and pacify my pride, I also wanted a friend who was not a therapist or in some way connected to Justin. I hoped another homeschool mom might be able to offer me not only the answers I sought but also some much needed encouragement and support. Justin received a weekly session of PT, OT, and speech in addition to skilled nursing service once a week, which provided our home with frequent visitors. But I was still lonely for friends.

It was out of character for me to initiate a friendship, but I was desperate, so I decided to take a chance and give Michelle a call. Tentatively I dialed the number. "Hello, Michelle, this is Sheila Campbell. I don't know if you remember me, but I am a friend of Sylvia Martin. She introduced us a couple of years ago. . . . Um . . . I was just wondering if you were still homeschooling and if maybe we could get together sometime." The words spilled awkwardly off my tongue and I paused, hoping I didn't sound too foolish.

"Of course, I remember you!" Michelle replied cheerfully. "You're the one with the three little boys. How is your son? Sylvia told me a little about what happened. Is he better? Are you still homeschooling?" Thus began a conversation that lasted over an hour and a friendship that would last a lifetime.

I soon discovered that Michelle also had a strong desire to connect with other homeschool moms to share information and encouragement. She had considered trying to start a homeschool group for a couple of years and had even attended some leadership workshops in Plano to gather information on how to form a group, but life circumstances had prevented her from moving forward with her efforts. My phone call to Michelle in mid-March of 1994 had caught her in the middle of a move. She was moving from their home east of Hale Center to Plainview (a larger town in the area). My recent move had brought us about fifteen miles closer to Plainview as well. We both considered our new locations to be providential.

Although she had heard from Sylvia about the complications that occurred during Justin's surgery, Michelle did not know about the addition of Jennifer to our family. I was surprised and excited to discover that Michelle and her husband, Steve, had also added a new baby girl to their family. Before we ended our call, the two of us had decided to try to unite the homeschool families in the Plainview area with the goal of starting a homeschool support group. Our first event would be a skating party. Michelle knew a few other homeschool families. She also planned to post notices about the party at the library. I would set up the event with the skating rink and address invitations to the small list of homeschoolers Michelle knew since she was still in the process of moving.

What started as a small gathering of homeschoolers quickly expanded as more names were added to our invitation list almost daily. On the day of the skating party, almost twenty families showed up. I had no idea there were that many homeschoolers in our area. I gathered a list of names and addresses and was soon sending out a short monthly newsletter to our list. To my surprise, Robby supported me and encouraged fellowship with our new friends. The boys quickly made friends and were soon telling stories about the things they were doing with their "school" friends to grandparents and at family gatherings, which helped silence some of the questions about socialization.

Although it was difficult to add a newsletter to my already overflowing schedule, it gradually became a source of healing for my own heart as I began to include little notes of encouragement in the newsletter. These words of encouragement to other homeschool moms were letters to myself as I wrote about the things the Lord revealed to me as I taught my children. My Heavenly Father was reaching down in love and using the scriptures and Bible stories in Jacob's curriculum and the deep desire he had given me long before Justin's surgery to spend time with and enjoy my children. The opportunity to teach them lessons from the Bible along with their academics began healing my broken heart. Though I still felt confused and at times lost as anger and frustration continued to pour from my mouth and heart more often than I wanted to admit, God no longer seemed so distant. He was right there in the midst of our school, and I found myself dwelling on the simple lessons of faith I was teaching to Jacob throughout the day. Many times I shared those lessons and others in the newsletter.

God had not stepped in and rescued me from my circumstances in the way I thought he should, and I still could not understand why he had allowed such a tragedy to occur, but I no longer felt abandoned. And while I still felt as though I were traveling in circles with a faith that was fickle, the scenery was a little greener and the path a little smoother each time. God was there in the stories he gave me to read and in the words he gave me to write. He had become real and tangible.

When Michelle and I finally hung up that first day, I not only had a new friend, but I had also gained a new purpose. My world had suddenly expanded beyond my little family. Michelle opened my eyes to a world I had limited experience with. Although they were not rich, she and Steve were able to do things I had never even considered.

Not long after our first skating party, Michelle called me one day. "Sheila, have you ever been to the homeschool book fair in Arlington?"

"No, I've never even heard about it."

"Would you like to go with me?" Michelle invited. "I think it would be a great opportunity for us to gather resources and information for our group as well as for our own kids." She had all the details: what it would cost to fly to Dallas and rent a car, hotel costs, and an estimate for meals. Since her daughter, Elizabeth, was only five months old, Michelle thought it would be better for both of us to be away from our families as little as possible, so she suggested flying down on a Friday morning and flying back on Saturday night. It was something I would have never considered on my own. I was thankful she made all the plans because I didn't have any idea how to plan such a trip. It was an event I would never forget.

After we lived with my parents for those few weeks, my mother had begun coming on a regular basis to help me with Justin and allow me a little time away to go get groceries. She had changed jobs again and was no longer working in Lubbock but was working for a homehealth agency in Plainview. When I told her about our plans for the Arlington trip, she offered to take off work for a day to stay with the kids and help care for Justin. She offered to stay all day until Justin went to bed. Although I worried about how Justin would do at night, I decided to go anyhow and let Robby take care of him.

I was so thankful for the opportunity. At the book fair, I found the encouragement I desperately needed. It was far more than information about curriculum, learning styles, and teaching methods. It seemed that in every workshop the speakers talked about incorporating education into everyday life and interweaving the Word of God and our Christian beliefs into every lesson. I discovered that homeschooling was more than just a method of education that allowed parents to spend more time with their children; it was a lifestyle choice.

One of the workshop speakers spoke on nurturing your child's heart. It was a workshop geared toward parents of preschool and kindergarten children, and I struggled to hold back my tears as she spoke. Many of the things she mentioned were things I once did with my boys before Justin had surgery. Things like reading to them and taking nature walks. I swallowed back painful memories of happy times spent with my beautiful little boys and found myself praying—begging—the Lord to show me how to recapture those times. I felt helpless to know how to include Justin in our lives, but I was determined not to leave him out. I so desperately wanted to enjoy my children, not just care for them but treasure each moment with them. What I didn't see was that as much as I wanted to treasure and enjoy every precious moment with my children God had so graciously given me, he wanted me to spend every precious moment loving and enjoying him. He was calling out and opening my heart to treasure the giver and not just the gifts.

Chapter 23

The Beginning of Balance

Why am I discouraged? Why is my heart so sad?
I will put my hope in God! I will praise him again—
my Savior and my God! Now I am deeply discouraged,
but I will remember you.
Psalm 42:5-6

Life was changing even though Justin's progress had slowed to a standstill. I was continually trying to find a balance that would allow me to care for both Justin and the rest of my household. During those first two years, Jacob and Jerrod had learned how to help me with the laundry, set the table, dust, and even run the vacuum. They kept their toys in order and put away their own clothes. I had come to rely heavily on their help, and regular tasks assigned to each of them had become part of their daily routine. Jacob would make all three beds in their room, and Jerrod would help get Jennifer dressed every morning. This allowed me the time I needed to get Justin up and ready for breakfast. Jacob was also in charge of Jennifer during mealtimes. He would cut up her food and make sure she had something to drink in her toddler cup while I fed Justin.

Robby rarely ate breakfast or supper with us, but he came home each day for lunch, our biggest meal of the day. I never asked him to help with Justin because I felt he needed to eat and get back to work. He never offered to help so he did not have much experience feeding Justin or helping at mealtime. Robby had been raised with the lady of the house taking care of all the household duties, and that way of life had prevailed during the earlier years of our marriage. However, while Robby assumed things could continue as they always had, his household changed around him. I did not know how to include him in changes I felt I could not prevent—changes he did not want. But with the boys helping with household tasks, I was able to incorporate more of Justin's care into our daily routine and find more time to spend with all of them.

After returning home from the Arlington book fair, I was determined to apply some of the things I learned in the workshops—especially the workshop on nurturing your children. I wanted to find some things I could do with everyone, including Justin. Justin had always loved music, and since his surgery, we had discovered it was the one stimulus he consistently responded to. I had purchased some scripture memory music to add to Justin's growing collection of children's praise songs, so I modified Jacob's school schedule and the simple IEP I kept for Justin to include music time. This made our music time together more official and less likely to be skipped because laundry or some other household chore took priority.

Every day the five of us gathered in the living room. I

would stand Justin up in front of me, supporting him in a standing position, while Jacob operated the tape player and we listened and sang together. We would make up motions to some of the songs, and I would stretch Justin's arms or sway with him back and forth. Without a whimper, Justin tolerated motions he normally met with cries of protest. He would even smile and sometimes squeal with delight as we all lifted our voices in song. It was easy to tell which songs were his favorites.

Jacob, Jerrod, and I were able to memorize several passages of scripture as we listened to GT and the Halo Express. Singing praise songs along with the Donut Man began to fill our home and our hearts with praise. As music became a part of our daily routine and something we all shared instead of just a way to entertain Justin, it changed the atmosphere of our home. Those simple songs of thanksgiving and praise gradually became much more than just words put to music; they became the prayer of my heart. I discovered that those simple songs designed for children had an amazing power to soften grief and soothe raw emotions. They opened a channel of praise that mere words alone had not been able to unlock.

The music also had a noticeable effect on Jacob and Jerrod. They were happy and content. We discovered music could soothe restless spirits and calm ruffled tempers. It could also ease worried minds and comfort wounded hearts. As we lifted our voices each morning, my heart began to heal and the boys' hearts began to blossom. Moment by moment the music took our eyes off our circumstances and turned our focus on praise to God. Through music, peace found its way into our home once more.

As I attempted to rebuild our family unit and reunite the bond we once took for granted, I began looking for ways our entire family could spend time together doing something fun. Jacob and Jerrod had received new bicycles for Christmas, and by spring they both could ride without training wheels. Watching them ride around the farm in the evenings had motivated Robby to fix up his own bicycle and join them. Inspired by some bicycle carts I had seen, I asked Robby if he thought he could design something Justin could ride in that we could attach and pull behind one of our bikes.

After some thought, Robby designed a cart for Justin using some wide solid rubber wheels with spokes similar to bicycle wheels. He mounted Justin's unused car seat, which had a five-point harness, onto the frame of the cart and tilted the seat slightly in an inclined position. He even made the angle of the incline adjustable. We had never been able to use the seat because Justin needed to be tilted back when traveling, but it was perfect on the new cart. The cart had one rear axle, and the front of the cart attached to brackets mounted on both my bicycle and Robby's so either of us could pull Justin. We purchased a baby seat for Jennifer, which we also mounted on my bicycle.

For the first time since Justin's surgery, we were able to enjoy spending time together as a family. We would often bike in the evenings, riding up turn rows to watch irrigation water run down them, admiring growing crops, or riding down dirt roads as the sun dipped low in the sky.

"I'll race you!" Jerrod called out to his brother as his little legs peddled furiously down the dirt road, leaving a smoke trail of dust behind.

"You got a head start," Jacob protested as he lifted himself off the bicycle seat to apply more power to the pedals. "But I'm catching you!" he called out as he began to gain on his brother.

Suddenly both boys were engulfed in a cloud of dust as Robby passed them pulling Justin along behind him. Justin seemed unaffected by the rough ride and the dirt. "I'll race you both!" he challenged. Then he slowed his pace so his laughing little boys could catch up and once more gain the lead.

"We win!" Jacob and Jerrod cried out happily as they united as a team to defeat their challenger.

"No, Justin and I beat you first," he teased.

I watched from a distance and smiled as I trailed the racers, thankful for my ingenious husband and Justin's cart.

The only drawback to the new cart was the weight it added to the back of the bicycle. As it was mounted on a bicycle and Justin placed in it, someone had to hold down the front of the bike to prevent the front wheel from leaving the ground. This was especially true on my bicycle, which also had the additional weight of Jennifer's baby seat. When Robby wasn't there to pull Justin, it took both the boys to hold my bicycle steady while I loaded and buckled Justin and Jennifer into their seats. Then I had to ride leaning heavily on the front handlebars. If I sat up straight, I would find the front wheel leaving the ground, but somehow I managed to keep the bike going and both tires on the road.

Everyone, including Justin, thoroughly enjoyed our new pastime. Sometimes in the afternoons, the kids and I would bike up the turn row to where Robby was working and take him something to drink. It was not long before we added a basket behind Justin's seat to carry along drinks; however, since I had to keep enough weight on the front of my bicycle to keep it from tipping up, we were not able to stop for long. That was fine with Justin since he seemed to enjoy the movement of travel despite the bumpy roads.

Robby soon made further adjustments to Justin's cart (as we came to call it) that would allow it to be pulled around the farm like a wagon and still be used for biking. He added a long curved handle and a front wheel that would swivel, making steering the cart very easy and giving it a sharp turning radius. The handle was curved so it could be easily attached to a new bracket mounted behind the seat of my bicycle. This replaced the heavier metal bracket attached to the rear axle of the bicycle. The new handle could be attached to the bicycle with a simple drop of a pin, and the front wheel of the cart helped distribute the weight. Later Robby also added a bracket to Justin's cart to allow us to easily mount a tractor umbrella. This kept Justin's fair skin in the shade. We now had the perfect all-terrain vehicle for Justin.

Justin had always loved the outdoors, and it seemed he still enjoyed being outside. He not only tolerated the movement of the cart but also seemed to enjoy it even over rough terrain. He often tolerated long rides without a whimper and fussed and cried when it was time to come in. Justin's new cart opened up a door of opportunity for our family that would have never been possible otherwise. I practically skipped down the dusty turn row the first time we were able to once more enjoy a nature walk and examine the wonder of nature up close. The large rubber wheels, wagon design, and high clearance allowed the cart to maneuver over rough ground that would have been impossible to traverse with Justin's wheelchair. We also discovered that when used as a wagon, the grate on which Justin's feet rested was large

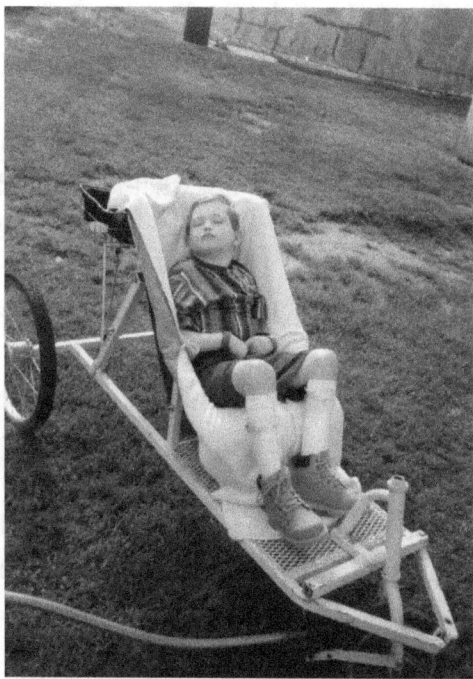

enough to allow Jennifer to sit between Justin's feet when her toddler legs became tired. She would often sit between his feet and put her little baby arms around the calves of his legs and hug his legs up close to her baby checks. If he fussed, she would gently pat his feet—though I doubt he felt much through his shoes and plastic AFOs.

That year my parents joined us on a family camping trip to the mountains. It had been three years since our family had gone on vacation, and I was excited to be returning to the mountains. We took Justin's cart along in the back of the pickup even though it took up an incredible amount of space. We could not have made the trip were it not for the cart. It became Justin's feeding chair as well as his primary means of travel. Although the trip was not unpleasant, it was very difficult to care for Justin. I felt as though caring for Justin and Jennifer kept my mother and me continually busy. I did not voice my thoughts to either Robby or my parents, but when we returned, I decided I did not want to attempt any more overnight trips with Justin—it was just too difficult. A vacation with Justin was just not what I had anticipated.

However, daily life at home gradually improved. I no longer felt as though I were caught in a whirlwind of overwhelming responsibilities and spinning helplessly out of control. Although I found little joy in the routine aspects of Justin's care, I no longer felt as though they were robbing me and keeping me from my other children. They were once more a part of my daily life and no longer left to themselves to pass the day. My days were slowly being filled once more with pleasurable moments spent with them. I felt as though God was returning my children to me, and they were the light of my life.

I remember reading *Walden* by Henry David Thoreau in high school. I had been deeply touched by his love of nature and his determination to "live life deliberately." I wanted to live life deliberately, and Justin's surgery had forced on me duties, responsibilities, and burdens I had neither asked for nor wanted. But they were duties I could not shake. Shouldering them had weighed me down and made life almost unbearable. Now, two years later, I felt life was finally slowing down enough to allow me to breathe deep, shoulder my burden, and move on, taking each deliberate step. No longer was I tumbling forward without any control.

Although I saw my children as a gift from the Lord and was enjoying their presence more each day, I still did not see how much I depended on them for my joy and happiness. They returned the love I showered on them with their words, actions, and companionship. Their very lives gave me hope for the future. Justin, however, could not return my love with words nor deeds, and the burden of his care often seemed so heavy. I no longer felt void of any feelings toward him. I did love him, but I struggled to accept that our relationship would now be one of continued unreturned and unrewarded service on my part and receiving on his part. Parents never want to admit they love their child as much for the child's potential as for who the child is at the moment, but I was beginning to understand I loved my children for the future joys our relationship may bring as well as the pleasures their fellowship provided in the present. I had put my faith for future happiness in my children.

However, the Lord was continuing the gentle process of prying my fingers loose from the gift and turning my eyes to the giver while still allowing me the pleasure of enjoying my children. I knew my children were a gift from God—a gift, not a burden—and much grief and confusion lingered within my heart. How could I enjoy Justin when he may never be able to return my affection or even offer gratitude for the service I was providing him? My desire to "live life deliberately" was a deep desire to glean pleasure from all the simple things God had created and had so abundantly bestowed on us, but it was also a selfish desire to accept only good from God's hand. A desire to love and serve only those things that would love and serve me in return. I wanted to serve the Lord but stubbornly clung to my desire to choose who and how I would serve.

I found myself often torn between hope and despair. Praise music opened the door for harmony and peace to once more enter our home. Justin's cart gave us the freedom to explore and enjoy the wonderful and beautiful world of nature. Although I worshipped and adored the creator in the music and in the wonder of creation, I still found more pleasure in the gifts than in the giver. My heart no longer felt estranged from my Heavenly Father. I had come to trust that my sin—which God was faithful to forgive—would not thwart his will. But it was still difficult to accept the tragedy that had befallen our family as part of God's plan for our lives. Although I would not admit it, I was still angry with God.

I continued to pray for Justin's healing, but I no longer knew if I should continue to hope that the Lord would bring healing to Justin's mind and body. And yet, the hope that God had something better for us—something better for Justin and therefore something better for me—was the only way I could find the faith to trust in God. This hope was like a sweet poison to my heart—this hope that Justin would eventually regain at least some of what he had lost. It was a hope that I could once more find pride and joy in all my children. A hope that I could receive from them some of the pleasure and unconditional love that I gave to them. It was faith for a future that was better than today. It never occurred to me that my fingers were wrapped so tightly around the gift of my children that I had allowed a pleasure in their love to fill God's place in my heart.

So, whenever Justin became irritable or cried uncontrollably, my growing fear that I would never again have pleasure in my relationship with him spilled out of my heart as anger. I wondered if I could ever let go of the hope that God would eventually restore something of what had been lost without completely letting go of my faith in a loving God. How could I trust a God who would take back the best gifts and leave me with a burdensome task in exchange? I could praise him as a sovereign God and trust in his sovereignty, but I found my belief in a loving God wavering. Although I had witnessed some difficult circumstances work for good in our lives, I was still skeptical of God's goodness.

≈ Chapter 24 ≈

Looking for Answers

I will look up to the mountains–does my help come from there?
My help comes from the Lord, who made heaven and earth!
Psalm 121:1-2

By the fall of 1994, we had become very involved in the new homeschool group that Michelle Cross and I had helped establish, Integrity Educators. Robby and I held the office of vice-president, while Steve and Michelle Cross together held the office of president. As we met new people and developed new friendships, I began to realize that we really didn't have many answers to the questions we received. People wanted to know what happened to Justin, what exactly caused his brain injury. They were not usually satisfied with the response that it was a complication of open-heart surgery.

We had begun to speculate by the time we left the hospital that Justin's brain damage was primarily the result of lack of oxygen that occurred when his cardiologist had removed him from the ventilator, but we were never told why his brain damage was so extensive. In rehab he was given the diagnosis of anoxic/hypoxic encephalopathy, which we quickly learned is a term that means brain damage due to lack of oxygen, but we were never given any clear answers on how this lack of oxygen occurred. Instead, we were given several *hypothetical suggestions* on how it *might* have occurred.

While Justin was in the ICU, we were told he had developed pneumonia shortly after he was re-intubated. I suspected that perhaps his lungs had collapsed, but my questions were never directly answered. Justin's cardiologist also told us before he left the ICU that the damage may have occurred the night after surgery, that perhaps he had a stroke, but we were never given any specifics explaining why his cardiologist thought that may have occurred. We knew Justin had taken a turn for the worse during that first night following his surgery and were told that a bad blood transfusion had been a contributing factor, but we were never given any other specific answers.

For the first two years after Justin was released from the hospital, our family was merely surviving. Knowing exactly how and why Justin was brain damaged did not seem to matter much. The fact was, he was brain damaged, and we would have to learn how to care for him. Knowing how it occurred would not change the situation, and I did not have the mental energy to spend time analyzing the traumatic and hazy events following his surgery or trying to make sense of the vague answers we had been given. It took every ounce of my strength just to get through each day.

But as I began to evaluate what we had put together on our own—our own speculations about what happened and how it occurred—Robby and I decided we would like to know if our hypothesis was correct. After Justin had been in the ICU for several weeks, we had become familiar with his chart and could do a decent job of interpreting the information recorded there, so we decided to see if we could get a copy of Justin's medical records. It seemed that whatever happened occurred sometime within the first three days following surgery.

Making a trip to Lubbock was a major event for us. When Justin had a doctor appointment, I usually went straight to the appointment and then returned straight home because of Justin's tendency to become over-stimulated and irritable. It was also difficult to find a place to comfortably feed or change him. If I went anywhere alone and left Justin and my other children in the care of my mother or mother-in-law or a homehealth nurse, I worried about him. I didn't want someone else to have to endure an afternoon of intense crying, so I would do my errands as quickly as possible. Because it was close and convenient, we now did all our business and shopping in Plainview, which was less than ten miles away.

Despite the inconvenience, I decided to make a trip to Lubbock to see if I could get a copy of Justin's medical records. At least we might have some answers to the questions people often asked about the tragic events that led to his brain damage.

My first visit to the medical records department of the hospital proved to be completely unsuccessful. I approached the clerk behind the desk in the records department and cleared my throat. "Hello, I am Sheila Campbell. My son Justin Campbell had open-heart surgery here a couple of years ago. I would like to get a copy of his medical records."

The clerk looked up and asked, "What were the dates of his stay? His name is Justin Campbell?"

"Yes, Justin Campbell. He was admitted May 5, 1992."

"I'll be right back," she said as she looked at her computer. Then she turned to head down one of the aisles behind her where colored files filled rows of floor to ceiling shelves.

She returned empty-handed. "Mrs. Campbell, your son's file is very thick. We charge per page, and by the look of his file, it may cost over a hundred dollars to make you a copy. Are you sure you want one?"

"Well, I really just want a copy of his records from May fifth to May tenth. Could you just copy those records?"

"Just a minute and I'll pull them." She returned in a few moments looking perplexed. "We don't seem to have a record of those dates. Are you sure that was when he was admitted?"

"Yes, I am absolutely certain about the dates," I assured her.

"Okay. Well, sometimes those files can get a little jumbled. If you want to check back in a few days, I'll make a note and try to find the records for those dates."

So I left with more questions than answers.

A few weeks later, I decided I would try again to get a look at Justin's medical records. This time I called the records department of the hospital so they would have plenty of time to find the records I was requesting, but when I got to the hospital, they did not have them for me. The woman I spoke to tried to convince me that if I decided to purchase the complete medical file for Justin, she was sure it included a copy of his ICU stay. She was still certain the file had just been misplaced. I did not feel we had that much money to spend, so I again left empty-handed and confused.

As I headed down the hall toward the parking garage, one of the hospital employees I had seen in the records department, but not spoken to, caught up with me.

"Mrs. Campbell?" she asked. "I'm sorry, but I couldn't help but overhear your request for your son's records." She continued in a quiet but urgent tone. "I remember your little boy. How is he?"

She must have thought I looked surprised, so she added, "He had brain damage while he was in the hospital, right?"

"Yes," I said. I was surprised that someone in the records department would know about Justin, much less personally remember him. "Did you . . . were you . . . working in the ICU or rehab or somewhere caring for him while he was here?"

"No, I never worked directly with your son, but there weren't many hospital employees working here at the time who didn't hear about what happened. I'm surprised you didn't request his records a long time ago." She lowered her voice and continued, "If you want my advice—off the record of course—I would advise you to get a lawyer and have your lawyer request your son's records. You may get want you want that way."

Before I could reply, she turned and headed back down the hallway. "I'd better get back. Good luck."

I went home upset and confused. All we wanted were some clear answers about what had happened; I wasn't sure how I felt about getting a lawyer. I felt certain we wouldn't get any answers from a lawyer without being willing to file suit against Justin's doctor and perhaps the hospital. In my heart, I wrestled with a question: "Is it right to file suit?" I was sure no one had deliberately injured Justin, but were Justin's brain injuries the result of carelessness or perhaps prideful actions? And if so, would we be justified in suing?

Robby and I spent some time discussing whether we should find a lawyer. Neither of us knew how to even start looking for one. While we deliberated, harvest time came and went and soon the holidays were once more on us, so we dropped the discussion. But the topic would soon resurface.

⌒ Chapter 25 ⌒

A Handicapped Heart

─────────────────────

*I had to talk as though you belonged to this world
or as though you were infants in the Christian life. I had to
feed you with milk, not with solid food, because you weren't
ready for anything stronger. And you still aren't ready,
for you are still controlled by your sinful nature.*
1 Corinthians 3:1-3

Christmas 1994 was Justin's third Christmas after the tragic event that forever changed our lives, but the holidays had not gotten any easier. When the boys were still just babies, Robby and I had established our own holiday tradition of celebrating our own family Christmas on December 23. This was primarily because we typically spent most of the twenty-fourth with Robby's family and the twenty-fifth with mine. Since we lived just a few miles from both sets of parents, we always attended both family celebrations. We jokingly called it our three-day Christmas marathon.

Our own family celebration was always relaxed and fun.

The kids opened presents in the morning, and at lunch, we enjoyed a big meal I had worked on for several days. Justin was usually more irritable in the afternoons and seemed to do better when he was allowed to sit quietly after lunch. Jennifer was always a happier toddler after a nap, so both she and Justin were able to have their quiet nap times while the boys played with their new toys. Supper was a simple meal of leftovers followed by an early bedtime because of the hectic schedule ahead of us for the next two days. After everyone was in bed, I rocked Justin while Robby and I watched a movie together.

However, spending Christmas with either of our parents was not nearly as calm and peaceful. I packed a bag for both Jennifer and Justin a couple of days in advance so I wouldn't have to worry about it while we enjoyed our own family Christmas. Doing it early also gave me opportunity to add things as they came to mind. The Campbell family was growing rapidly and spouses and grandchildren quickly filled the old farmhouse where Robby grew up. I loved visiting with everyone and seeing all the kids, but Justin was easily over-stimulated and it was difficult to find a place for him to sit comfortably. Since Justin ate in his little recliner at home and it was too bulky to bring along, feeding him was a challenge. Carrying him down narrow hallways to find a private place to change him was difficult and tiresome. Sometimes Robby offered to help with his care when we were in family settings, but since he rarely helped at home, I was usually uncomfortable and nervous accepting his assistance. I felt awkward and embarrassed to insist on taking care of Justin myself, and so his offer just added to the tension I felt.

Christmas day at my parents' home was a little better

simply because my mother made a tremendous effort to handle as much of Justin's care as possible to allow me a break from the daily routine and let me enjoy the holiday. But since she was the hostess, this put a lot of stress on her as she tried to prepare the meal, serve, and make sure everyone was comfortable, and I was hesitant to relinquish any of his care to anyone else. My family was smaller and for many years my children were the only grandchildren so the activity level was lower and Justin was not as easily over-stimulated. But nothing is quite like home and I was always relieved when the holidays were over.

⌒

As the holiday season passed and a new year began, Justin began having more seizures. Since he had started seizing, his seizures had never been completely under control. He had auditory-triggered seizures daily, but I began to notice additional seizure activity following an auditory-triggered tonic or clonic seizure (sometimes referred to as a grand mal seizure). When he had these seizures, his body would stiffen and then rapidly shake. His arms would draw up close to his body and his breathing would become rapid and shallow. They usually lasted less than a minute and most of the time Justin would emerge from them stiff and crying.

At first the additional smaller seizures—referred to as petite mal or absentee seizures—were barely detectable—just a few eye blinks that caught my attention. A few minutes after he had calmed down from an auditory-triggered seizure, I would notice his eyes blink with the unusual rhythm of a seizure. Occasionally I could also detect a slight twitch to his right hand.

In the beginning, there were only a few eye blinks and then nothing, so my suspicions that he may have had another small seizure were difficult to prove. However, the smaller seizures gradually increased in duration, and within a few weeks, I knew Justin was seizing several hours a day. I visited with his neurologist, and he arranged for Justin to be admitted for a 24-hour EEG scan. The scan confirmed my observations—Justin was seizing almost continually.

So began another battle with seizure medication. The first step was to look at Justin's regular blood work and determine if his Depakote could be increased. Unfortunately, we could not increase the Depakote, so the alternative was to add an additional seizure medication. One at a time, we tried six more seizure medications and I kept a record of his growing list of allergies. Justin would tolerate each new medication for about a week, and then he would break out in a rash indicative of an allergy. The only other seizure medication he was not allergic to was the Klonopin, which we had tried once before right after he came home from the hospital. The results were the same. Although the Klonopin helped control the seizures, it made him very sleepy and relaxed his tone to the point that he had difficulty bearing his own weight.

I was at a loss. If we kept Justin on the Klonopin, any progress he might make in his physical therapy would come to a standstill or he might even regress. However, we couldn't let him just continue to seize all day. The increase in seizure activity was making him increasingly irritable and hypersensitive. Once again, Justin had become the focal point of my day. Between seizures, I spent most of the day rocking him and trying to help him relax his high tone. When he was seizing, I felt guilty leaving him in a chair and letting him seize, but I also felt I had to take advantage of the time to get my daily household tasks accomplished. Jacob's schoolwork was temporarily put on hold and I employed both Jacob and Jerrod to help me with daily household tasks.

Lisa Dillard, Justin's primary nurse, mentioned she had heard of a pediatric neurologist in Lubbock who was experimenting with a new diet to help control seizures and was having some success. I thought it would be worth a try. I was happy with Justin's neurologist, but I was not ready to sacrifice any possible advances in physical therapy for seizure control.

I made a few phone calls and we were soon in the office of a new neurologist discussing the Ketogenic diet and how it worked. The diet was very difficult to maintain. It required that all food be measured and was made up mainly of protein and fat with little to no carbohydrates or sugar. The diet was initiated with a three-day fast, which I knew would be difficult for Justin because of his meds. The diet worked much like fasting and tricked the body into burning fat for energy instead of carbohydrates. This created a chemical change in the brain that helped control seizures.

The Ketogenic diet proved to be even more difficult than I had imagined, but it worked. By the time Justin completed his three-day fast, he was no longer seizing continually. Much to my disappointment, he continued to have the auditory-triggered, tonic-clonic, seizures, but they were no longer followed by a series of absentee or petit mal seizures, so his neurologist considered the diet a success.

However, the diet presented new problems. Because he was on a puree diet, Justin's meals were difficult to prepare and I had considerable trouble getting him to eat. He not only disliked the texture of many of his meals, but it was obvious he also disliked the taste. I hated forcing him to eat, and I felt awful removing one of the few pleasures he could enjoy. I would often skip meals because I felt guilty enjoying a meal when he could not so our mealtime battles soon caused both of us to lose weight. It was also difficult to get Justin to drink enough liquids to stay hydrated since he had difficulty swallowing water or other thin liquids. More than once, he was hospitalized to rehydrate him with IV fluids when routine lab work revealed severe dehydration. Because IV fluid contained dextrose—a form of sugar—a hospital stay was usually followed by increased seizure activity. We would return home and have to start the diet all over again with a three-day fast.

Before we started the Ketogenic diet, I would give Justin his Depakote capsules tucked into a bite of oatmeal, which he swallowed without any difficulty since he rarely attempted to chew. The new diet consisted mostly of shakes made with cream (instead of milk) or butter and ground beef or some other rich, thick concoction. To get his Depakote down, I would shoot the capsule to the back of his throat by pinching it between my fingers and then follow with a sip of water. The capsule had to land just right at the back of his tongue—too far back and he could choke, not far enough and he would try to chew and crush it with his teeth, releasing its bitter contents. For several months I was the only one able to master giving Justin his medication. Once again, only I could feed him.

Although Justin's seizures were better, he continued to

be extremely irritable. The chloral hydrate, a mild sedative Dr. Linton provided us with, had always been difficult to administer. It was a bitter liquid that had a slight burning sensation when swallowed—much like alcohol. I had to be very careful when giving it to Justin or he would choke, and aspiration was always a possibility. Although it was difficult, I had mastered the technique required to give Justin the bitter liquid slowly enough that he could swallow it and yet quickly enough that he would not cough and spit it out; however, the medication also had a tendency to upset Justin's stomach. This tendency was magnified by the new diet, so frequently he would take the chloral hydrate down as the last step in his evening mealtime only to have everything come back up— which also increased his chances of aspiration.

Preparing Justin's food, feeding him, and continually dealing with his upset stomach soon began to wear on my nerves. Once more I was struggling with bouts of anger and resentment toward Justin, especially when I felt I was under pressure to get a meal on the table or something else required my immediate attention and his continual crying was almost unbearable. But my anger was also mixed with a feeling of resignation that hung like a dark cloud over me. I was beginning to lose hope. I was finally resigning myself to caring for Justin forever. Justin's future seemed dark and dismal: a life without communication or joy, constantly fighting pain and high tone with very little progress to show for all the struggle and work. A living death that would trap me beside him. It was a future without hope and I found myself praying that the Lord would take Justin if he did not plan to heal him. If it were not for my other children, I would have prayed for my own death, but I knew they needed me and I could not bear to leave them. Then guilt and grief would come crushing down on me and I would drop to my knees and ask forgiveness for such a selfish prayer. What I really wanted was for the Lord to remove this trial. I did not want to raise a handicapped son. I wanted my whole and perfect little boy back. I was angry that God had taken the child I once had and guilty for feeling selfish and angry.

One day after an angry outburst, I found myself locked in the bathroom on my knees in tears, crying out to God in a prayer of bitter complaint. "Oh God," I cried, "I don't know if I can handle this. It is so unfair to have a child who will never grow up, never feed himself, and never eat from our table." I begged, "Please, please, heal him and give him the ability to communicate and feed himself. Please help him learn to do something—anything."

Instantly, Paul's words to the Corinthian church came to mind: "I had to talk as though you belonged to this world or as though you were infants in the Christian life. I had to feed you with milk, not with solid food, because you weren't ready for anything stronger. And you still aren't ready, for you are still controlled by your sinful nature. "

I suddenly realized that *I* was the one who was handicapped. *I* was the one still unable to eat meat from the table. It was *my* heart that was immature and weak. *I* was the one who needed to be helped and healed.

I had been trying to squelch and hide my selfishness and anger rather than admit my feelings and surrender them to my Heavenly Father, who was waiting patiently to help me. I knew my thoughts were selfish and that Justin was suffering far more than I. I began to earnestly seek the Lord in prayer and ask him to remove my anger. I would look at my young son and search my heart to find feelings of love and compassion, only to discover to my dismay that my heart seemed empty. I wanted to love my son; I wanted to feel compassion and sympathy, not anger. If it was the Lord's plan for my life to live it in service to my son—if I was to be a martyr (as I saw it) and live a life void of joy—then I wanted to sacrifice that service without anger or resentment. I resolved to be obedient without complaint, and I prayed for the love and compassion that I did not feel.

What I did not understand then was that letting go of my anger would also require me to let go of my expectations and accept what the Lord had for me. This journey of letting go and learning to love unselfishly would be a long, hard road. I would travel much of it on my knees in prayer. I alternated between begging God to heal Justin and remove this burden from our lives . . . and begging God to help me control my anger and give me love and compassion for my son.

Chapter 26

Growing Gratitude for Roads Not Traveled

The Lord says, "I will guide you along the best pathway for your life. I will advise you and watch over you."
Psalm 32:8

Summer 1995 was difficult. Justin's new diet added additional limitations to our participation in any functions outside our family. However, when Steve and Michelle Cross added a new baby girl to their family, Robby and I assumed the office of president in the local homeschool support group. Since it was difficult for me to leave Justin and I needed to be available to help give him his medication, I began to host group events at our house. My mother was always willing to come and help with Justin—I could never have managed without her assistance.

I was so blessed by the fellowship of the women I met through the homeschool group. I no longer felt alone as I began building lasting friendships with these extraordinary women of faith. It was always such a pleasure to host afternoon events at the house and to enjoy the fellowship of women while the children played. These women shared a love for the Lord and a love and commitment to their families and children that was edifying. It filled the well of my heart with encouragement at a time when all else seemed dreary. My life is a lasting testament to the mentoring of these women.

Janet Norton, although not associated with our local homeschool group, was another homeschool mom who forever impacted my life. She and her precious family, whom we met the year after Justin's surgery, continued to plan visits around Janell's appointments in Lubbock. I was inspired by the relationship her children had with Janell and always convicted by their willingness to help with Janell's care. They were so loving and gentle with her, and I knew that their attitude toward their sister was a reflection of their parents. I often prayed that my children could someday emulate their example.

As summer passed and a new school year approached, we discovered that Justin no longer qualified for home health assistance because of changes in the program. At first, I was concerned about how we would continue to provide him with the therapy he needed, but Lisa Dillard was so helpful. She knew how to request services from the public school, and I soon discovered that the school was quite willing to continue to pay for Justin to receive therapy services at home. Since Pediatric Therapy Services, the company through which Justin was receiving services, contracted with the school, none of Justin's therapists changed and his therapy remained the same.

However, since Justin no longer qualified for skilled nursing, Lisa would no longer be visiting or overseeing his care. Our whole family would miss her. Before she left, Lisa helped us apply for social security disability benefits. We received a check for back payments from the time Justin was first considered eligible. This helped us purchase a suburban that had four bucket seats. Now Justin no longer had to ride in the front. The middle bucket seats were adjustable just like the front seats, so the seat could be tilted back, and the seat belt helped secure Justin in place. The rear bench seat could easily fold down into a small bed; this provided a place to change Justin when traveling. It was exactly what we needed.

Lisa also helped us apply for respite care, and Justin easily qualified. However, although the funds were available, finding someone willing to come and learn Justin's care was not easy. We found it difficult to find someone who was trustworthy, dependable, hardworking, and willing to serve Justin and try to meet his needs. My mother continued to be my most dependable help as we went through a series of caretakers.

As the year passed and fall faded into winter, Justin continued with the diet. It did help with seizure control, but he continued to struggle with dehydration. Since we had become actively involved in the homeschool group, my children—especially the boys—had made several friends. However, I soon discovered that whenever children play with other children, they are eventually introduced to a variety of colds and viruses. I was extremely cautious about exposing my kids to any kind of illness, and it frustrated me when some of my friends did not appreciate my caution. They simply could not know or understand how difficult it was to care for Justin when he was sick. His daily care was difficult enough without adding a cold or virus, and a simple cold could quickly become serious for Justin.

One night I awoke to the awful sound of Jennifer

throwing up in her bed. I sat up and suddenly I too felt queasy, but I managed to get Jennifer up, bathed, and her bed changed before I was doubled over in the bathroom. I had just laid my hot forehead briefly on the cold porcelain of the bathtub, relieved that Jennifer was once more sleeping soundly, when I heard Justin coughing. Instinctively, I knew he was also sick.

Weak and shaking, I managed to grab a towel and sit him up in bed enough to keep him from aspirating. Then in the dark of the night, I got him up and into a warm tub. I had just gotten him cleaned up and wrapped in a towel when another wave of nausea hit me and I had to leave him wrapped in a towel sitting in the recliner while I made another run to the bathroom. Using every ounce of strength I had, I managed to get Justin dressed and reclining in the living room with a large towel draped over him.

Between waves of nausea, I was able to help Jennifer again, settling her in the living room with Justin, where it was easier to care for the both. Then I put both Jennifer's and Justin's sheets and bedding into the washing machine. Finally, so weak that I was having difficulty walking, I collapsed on the living room floor and slept soundly on the hard floor for a few hours.

By morning, Jennifer was feeling better, and I tucked her into bed where she slept for several hours. I no longer felt nauseous, but I was incredibly weak. I was worried that Justin would quickly become dangerously dehydrated, but I did not think I had the strength to get him to the doctor and I was too proud to call someone to help us. Since Justin could so easily become dehydrated on the diet, Dr. Linton had inserted an NG tube (a feeding tube through his nose into his stomach) for us several times to avoid a hospital stay. I had watched her carefully as she inserted the tube, and she had always been kind enough to explain each step as she performed the procedure. We had been given an extra tube to use in case of an emergency while Justin was still receiving skilled nursing services.

Driven by fear and desperation, I retrieved the tube. With trembling hands, I carefully inserted the tube down Justin's nose, keeping to the back of his throat to avoid his airway and praying all the while for help. I was surprised at how easily it went into place. After I had it in place, I listened with a stethoscope as I forced a little air down the tube to see if I could determine the positioning. The first time Dr. Linton used an NG tube for Justin, she X-rayed him to make sure it was positioned correctly and the right length. All subsequent tubes were cut to the exact same length, including the extra tube we had at home.

I was afraid to use the tube and afraid not to, so I cautiously poured a few ounces of Sprite down the tube. No coughing, nothing—Justin did not even wake up. I continued to pour a few ounces down every couple of hours until Justin seemed to be fully recovered. He had a good cough reflex, so after the first couple of ounces, I was confident the tube was positioned correctly . . . and so very grateful.

I was able to doze some while Jennifer and Justin slept. By the end of the day (due largely to the use of the NG tube) we were all feeling much better, but the fear of "what if" I had not put the tube in correctly lingered on my mind for several days. It made me wonder if I believed more in chance and happenstance than in God's divine providence and care. And I wondered at my own lack of faith despite my desire to believe.

Christmas that year found Justin once more sick and dehydrated. On December 23, the day of our family Christmas, right after the kids finished opening their gifts, I left a turkey in the oven, my own presents unopened under the tree, and took Justin in to see Dr. Linton. Once more she inserted an NG tube so I could keep Justin hydrated and sent us home as quickly as possible. She was always so considerate of his hypersensitivity to the clinic environment and seemed to allot us special consideration by getting us in and out of the clinic as quickly as possible. I had considered inserting the tube myself, but my ever-present struggle with fear and doubt had made me reconsider, and I was thankful the hospital was close and the visit was quick.

After Justin and I returned home, we spent the day in our usual manner enjoying the traditional holiday fare for lunch. Justin was unusually quiet and sleepy, so the afternoon passed uneventfully. The next morning, we loaded kids and gifts for the family and prepared to head to Robby's parents for day two of our Christmas marathon. Although I knew it would be difficult and would split my heart as well as my family's, I desperately longed to say home with Justin. I wasn't sure which was more difficult: to separate my family at events in which other families were complete or to attend as a family and pretend that our family was whole and normal.

Many times my mother kept Justin while the kids and I attended special events hosted by our homeschool group such as recital nights, play performances, and graduation or promotion celebrations. I was always thankful for the opportunity to get out and surrender Justin's care to my mother's capable hands for the evening, but at the same time, I felt torn because I had to leave him behind. I wanted to be with my other children and fully enjoy them. But I also wanted to be with Justin, and I felt as though I never could have both. The same was true when someone else would take my children to field trips and events and I stayed behind to care for Justin. I did not want to leave Justin nor did I want to miss sharing the experience with the kids, but Justin's sensitivity to stimuli and noise in addition to his other handicaps made most events uncomfortable and unpleasant for both of us.

As we loaded up the suburban that morning of December 24, I felt a strange sadness.

"Mama, where is Justin's bag?" Jacob asked as he helped load presents into the suburban.

"Mama is going to stay here with Justin today since he's not feeling well," Robby answered as he helped Jacob arrange his load in the back.

"But you're going to miss Christmas." Jacob looked perplexed.

"We enjoyed a nice Christmas yesterday," I said, smiling down at him. "Justin and I will have a nice quiet day. I'll read him a story and we'll listen to Christmas music and maybe even watch a Christmas movie, so don't worry about us."

"I'll tell Justin a Christmas story at Mamma's," Jerrod offered as he helped buckle Jennifer in and then fastened his own seatbelt.

"I think Justin will rest better here. I don't think he will mind staying home since there are so many people at Mamma's," I responded, trying to reassure them.

"Are you sure you don't want to try it?" Robby asked. "We could come home early if we need to."

"No, I don't want you to miss out," I replied, trying to sound more cheerful than I felt. "Go and have a good time and tell everyone I said Merry Christmas."

I stood and watched them leave and then headed back inside where Justin sat in his recliner. Although this was our fourth Christmas since Justin's surgery, the reality that this was how it was always going to be had finally settled in. I wondered if I could handle the pain of watching everyone else grow up and change while Justin remained virtually the same. Christmas, particularly Christmas celebrations with extended family, had become one of the most difficult events of the year for me. Our family was different, I was different, and it was difficult to accept that family celebrations might not ever be the same again. Recognizing that my desire to stay home alone with Justin was stronger than my desire to celebrate with family made me realize how isolated I felt even when surrounded by family.

Justin's brain injury had changed our family in other ways too. The differences were subtle and I could not articulate exactly what had changed, but our family was different. I'm certain homeschooling contributed to those differences. Now that all the grandchildren were growing up and attending school, the different educational choice for our family made everyday conversation about our children a little more strained as each of us tried to be careful not to offend the other.

I was grateful beyond words for the new friends we had made in the homeschool community. They challenged my thinking and my Christian walk. Their influence had changed me for the better, I hoped. But as my family changed and I changed, I couldn't help but feel those differences were distancing me from Robby's family, and that saddened me. Our marriage was on shaky ground. Although I tried to keep our marital difficulties hidden, the strain on our marriage also created an invisible and imperceptible barrier between my in-laws and me. I knew they were not the ones who had changed—it was me—but I felt the loss deeply.

There were times, and the holidays were usually one of those times, when I couldn't help but wonder if we would still be homeschooling if it were not for Justin's brain injury. His loss not only kept me home but also provided us with some extra income from Justin's SSI check. Without the SSI check and Justin's need for continual care, I may have made different schooling choices.

We can never know the "what ifs" that lay on the roads not taken. Eventually—ever so slowly—I began to be grateful for the path that was mine to travel as the Lord filled my heart and mind with gratitude. I was grateful for the changes in my heart and in my beliefs. This was not a gratitude born out of duty, and I realized it was a gift, not anything I had managed to acquire on my own. I was beginning to see the good in some of the difficult things in my life and be truly thankful for the trials that revealed my depraved heart. Often in the past, it had been my habit to express thankfulness to God because I felt it was my Christian duty. Now I realized with brokenness that my gratitude also gave me a prideful sense of entitlement. My false piety was a way to try to subtly manipulate God. However, this new thankfulness was something I could not explain. As it began to fill my heart, the road that we left untraveled began to fade in the distance. I no longer wondered what that road might be like if Justin was not handicapped. I could no longer even *imagine* what it might be like, and I found I desired it less and less. I was surprised to find, in the midst of loneliness and grief, a tiny seed of genuine gratitude growing within my heart for a life so different and far more difficult than I had imagined.

☞ Chapter 27 ☜

A Renewed Search
for Answers

*The Lord is good and does what is right;
he shows the proper path to those who go astray.
He leads the humble in doing right, teaching them his way.
The Lord leads with unfailing love and faithfulness
all who keep his covenant and obey his demands.*
Psalm 25: 8-10

Winter passed along with the year. As the calendar turned, life remained much the same. Justin continued on the Ketogenic diet. The breakthrough petit mal seizures he had been having between or following an auditory-triggered grand mal seizure had stopped, and he had not had any breakthrough seizures for several months. However, the diet continued to be very difficult; Justin hated the food and he hated to eat. Although my mother could feed him, I was the only one who could give him his medication. Finding a good caregiver who could help me with Justin's care continued to prove to be a challenge. The one or two who were reliable and dependable did not stay long while others were either unreliable, untrustworthy, or both, and so I continued to care for Justin with little outside help aside from my mother.

When Justin did have a caregiver, I would use her to sit with him while the kids attended homeschool group activities and I ran errands and bought groceries. However, several times my mother dropped in unannounced while Justin was with a caregiver and discovered Justin left unchanged and crying on his bed while the caregiver was occupied with a movie or a book or on the phone. I was thankful for my mother's surprise visits and sometimes asked her to make them since they often confirmed my suspicions about the quality of the care he was receiving while we were away.

Between caregivers, my mother would stay with Justin when she wasn't working. Other times I would take him with us. That was difficult but at least I knew the quality of care he was receiving. Keeping Justin hydrated on the diet continued to be a problem, and I had to make sure I took time in the midst of our errands to give him several small sips of water.

By spring, Justin's neurologist decided to start weaning him off the diet to see how he responded. The first thing we added back to his diet was whole milk, which Justin easily swallowed. Justin liked milk and so he swallowed it without complaint. The milk was just slightly thicker than water, which made it easier to swallow. The addition of milk to his diet put an end to his hydration problems, while his seizures continued to remain in check. We hoped he would be able to gradually return to an unrestricted diet—at least as far as composition was concerned—without an increase in seizure activity.

One day in late spring a friend called and asked if she could stop by on her way back from town and let the boys play for a bit before heading home. Her older son and Jacob and Jerrod were close friends, and her younger son was autistic. Homeschooling while providing for our special needs children provided us plenty of topics for conversation.

I had felt a little nauseous for a couple of days but it was manageable, so I had ignored it. During her visit, I had a growing pain in my lower abdomen slightly to my right side. By the time we had said our good-byes and they were headed home, I knew something was wrong. I called the boys into the house and had them bathe early. Then I gave both Jennifer and Justin a bath, fixed a quick supper for the kids, and let them eat while I fed Justin. By the time I was finished feeding Justin and had given him his meds, Robby had come in for supper.

"Robby, I don't feel well at all," I said as he scrubbed his hands after a hard day of work.

"What's wrong?"

"I've been sick to my stomach for a couple of days, but I thought it would pass. Today I'm running a fever and I have a terrible pain on my right side."

He looked at me for a few seconds and then asked, "Do you think you need to go to the emergency room?"

"I hate to think what it may cost us, but yes, I do think I might have appendicitis. If you don't mind taking me, I'll call my mother and see if she can come stay with the kids."

"Is there anything I need to get for you?" Robby asked as he pulled his boots back on and put his billfold back in his pocket.

"I think I'm ready to go. I gathered up a few things earlier—just in case." I pointed to a small bag beside the door and Robby picked it up and carried it to the pickup. Nana was there within minutes and stayed the night with the kids while Robby stayed with me.

The doctor on call that night was Dr. Wilson, the same doctor whose son was killed years earlier when Justin was still very little. The death of his son was the first time I could ever remember as a parent facing the possibility that a child could die, but I think that loss now filled his heart with compassion for our family.

At 11:30 that night, my appendix was removed. The next morning, I was very sore but ready to go home. Dr. Wilson discharged me at noon, and I returned home to an empty house. Robby had to go check water on the farm while Justin, Jerrod, and Jennifer were all staying with my mother, who had taken a day off work to keep them. Jacob had been picked up that morning by friends to go take achievement tests, and they would bring him home later. For the first time since Justin's surgery and Jennifer's birth, all my children were elsewhere and I was alone. I wandered outside and sat down in the warm sunshine, allowing my thoughts to wander and trying to think about how different things would be if Justin had never been handicapped. I discovered I could not completely imagine away the life that was now mine.

That night the kids once again stayed with my mother, and Robby and I took advantage of a rare opportunity to go to Plainview and eat out. We rented a movie and came home to share a quiet evening. It was the only date night we had enjoyed since Justin's surgery almost four years earlier, and it was great for our shaky marriage. We found we still had things to talk about and enjoyed each other's company. It was a temporary lift to both of our spirits.

My mother brought the kids home the next morning

and stayed most of the day to help. It was Saturday and she was off for the weekend. She returned on Sunday morning to help me get Justin up and ready for the day. By Sunday evening I had resumed Justin's care and was once more lifting him despite the four-inch incision on my abdomen and the doctor's restrictions on my activity.

When I went to have the stitches removed the following week, Dr. Wilson was surprised at how quickly the incision had healed and attributed it to the fact that I was lean and in good shape because of the constant lifting Justin's care required. A few weeks later, I received a bill from him with a smiley face and a zero balance. At first I didn't understand, but then I realized he had written off the bill and had not charged me for his time or his talent. It was one of the most generous acts of kindness anyone had ever bestowed on us.

As summer wore on, Robby became increasingly restless and discontent with his job. I did not recognize it as depression, but I recognized the pattern and watched with growing concern as he began to stay up late and had difficulty sleeping. He had trouble focusing on his work and no longer found any pride or joy in his job. Although he was home more, he was distant and easily irritated. Robby had experienced downward turns in the past. Whenever he became despondent, I was not sure what to say or do to help him or encourage him—especially when I was also struggling to find joy in the simple pleasures of life and hope in a better tomorrow. The temporary boost that our marriage had received during my bout with appendicitis quickly disappeared, and the trough of despondence into which it fell grew ever deeper.

It had been two years since we first sought answers to

what happened to cause Justin such extensive brain damage. Increased seizures, the Ketogenic diet, homeschool group activities, and just daily living had interrupted our search for answers. But as fall settled across the south plains with its golden hues and another school year began, life once more settled into a regular schedule despite my growing anxiety about Robby's job. Justin had completely weaned off his Ketogentic diet and was back on his regular diet, which varied little but consisted mostly of oatmeal, baby food, pudding, mashed potatoes, Jell-O, and milk. He continued to have daily seizures, but the breakthrough petit mal seizures had not returned. Life for him had become a daily routine of AFO foot splints, soft neoprene thumb splints, physical therapy, and audio books and movies.

No longer overwhelmed with Justin's diet and repeated bouts of dehydration, I once more began to focus on finding some answers to the often asked questions about what went wrong with his surgery that had such devastating effects. Once more I tried to get records of Justin's ICU stay, and once more I was unsuccessful in my attempt. I discussed it with Robby, and we decided we would have to seek assistance if we ever wanted any clear answers.

Robby and I knew nothing about lawyers or how to find one, but his sister suggested a company in Lubbock. We decided to give them a call and see how much it would cost us to get some answers. When I contacted the firm and told them just a little bit about Justin and what we knew and what we speculated had happened, the firm wanted to know more. We set up an appointment to meet. Once we met with the lawyer, we immediately realized that to find answers, we would have to be willing to follow through with a suit. I really just wanted answers, but I knew we would not be able to get them without a lawyer. I also knew we could not afford a lawyer. By agreeing to file suit, we would allow them to recover the attorney's fees as part of the settlement or judgment. After much consideration, we agreed. Thus began the search for answers.

We were soon reviewing paperwork and preparing to file a lawsuit. The phone calls and paperwork were almost overwhelming to me, but the lawsuit seemed to give Robby a revived sense of purpose. I was thankful he was willing to handle so much of the work and correspondence with the attorneys. I worried that the time he was spending on the lawsuit would have a negative effect on his job, but by that point, communication between him and his boss was so tense, it was doubtful their relationship could be mended. Besides, the extra tasks seemed to revive his spirits, and so I was thankful for them.

⚛ Chapter 28 ⚛

Lessons in Unconditional Love

Now, most people would not be willing to die for an upright person, though someone might perhaps be willing to die for a person who is especially good. But God showed his great love for us by sending Christ to die for us while we were still sinners.
Romans 5:7–8

While Robby focused on the lawsuit and worked to bring in the harvest, I enjoyed the changing season. Fall and the cooler sunny days were my favorite time of the year to take our classroom outside and go on nature walks with the kids. Justin's cart now made that a possibility, and we spent many afternoons on the dusty farm roads watching crops mature for harvest, collecting leaves, and examining bugs and various wondrous aspects of creation. As we walked and spent time studying and talking about the miracles of the world God created, a childlike wonder and love for life and learning began to once more blossom in my heart.

"Hey, Mama, feel this," Jacob said as he held up a soft

ball of cotton he had carefully pulled from the boll. The fall sunlight highlighted the tints of red in his blond hair, and his interest in a boll of cotton reminded me that my "right-hand man" was still just a child.

"Look, I took the seeds out and I'm gonna plant them," Jerrod announced as he held out a handful of fuzzy seeds.

I took the cotton from Jacob and smiled at him as I gently rubbed my fingers over the cotton. Then I knelt down beside Justin's cart and put the soft cotton in his twisted hand.

"Do you feel the soft cotton in your hand, Justin?" I asked as I gently pressed his fingers around the wad of cotton. "Jerrod is going to plant some of the cotton seeds and we'll see if they grow."

Kneeling there on the dusty dirt road between the fields beside Justin's cart as the late afternoon sun sank lower in the west, I watched my curious children explore and learn about the world in which they lived. At that moment, life was good. Joy and peace were slowly returning and overflowing out of my life and into the lives of my children. Yet few things in life change instantly, and Justin continued to have episodes of irritability that were difficult for me to handle. When he was inconsolable, I always experienced an internal battle with my anger and frustration, but my heart was growing soft toward my son. I had begun to recognize that many times his irritability was a sign that he was either over-stimulated or uncomfortable. I was much better at interpreting his cries and whimpers and could sometimes manage to comfort him or reposition him so he was more comfortable and his tight muscles relaxed before his cries got out of control.

Although my heart now looked on my son with far more compassion, there were still times when I ignored his cries of discomfort and made him suffer through weight bearing and physical therapy. I knew it was painful for him, but I clung to the hope that he would continue to make progress even if it was in tiny increments so I continued to aggressively push his physical therapy. However, whenever I sat down to write his IEP for the year and realistically evaluated his progress, I was forced to see he had simply maintained what little he gained through that first difficult year. But still I buried that reality deep within my heart and refused to acknowledge it.

Instead of accepting the child I had been given and loving him despite his handicaps, I continued to cling to the hope that someday the door to his inner thoughts would open and he would once more be able to communicate with his family and the world around him. His only consistent attempt at communication was through crying, but I was determined that would change. Although Justin could bear weight when held in an upright position and step with his right leg when prompted, we could not get him to attempt to use a foot switch as a means of communication. The same was true with his right arm. He could use his arm and the back of his hand, which was turned in sharply at the wrist, to swipe at his nose when it obviously itched. But we could never get him to consistently try to operate a simple switch to turn on a tape player or a message board though we tried a variety of switches and incentives. It seemed his muscles could respond instinctively, but he either could not purposely control them or could not cognitively think through the process of attempting to control them. I could never determine the truth to my complete satisfaction, but I could not stop hoping that buried deep within was some remnant of the child I once knew. Nevertheless, my persistent need to change him—to improve him—was often like a poison that fueled my frustration and anger.

One day I was particularly frustrated with Justin after desperately trying to get him to respond or communicate. Hoping that he understood me, I had spent several minutes patiently talking to him and trying to explain what I wanted him to do. He had seemed unusually alert and appeared to be listening so I took advantage of the opportunity to give him several options for responding to simple yes or no questions. I offered suggestions for any possible means of communication that he might be able to control: blink an eye, twitch a finger, or wiggle a toe. But Justin's responses were inconsistent and my failure to make any progress made me want to cry. I desperately wanted to break down what seemed to be a wall that separated us.

There seemed to be more than just an infantile level of understanding somewhere within because he would laugh and squeal at his favorite movies and books. He obviously remembered them. I bought him the movie *Fievel Goes West* for his ninth birthday that year. I had taken the boys to see that movie just months before his surgery, and it was obvious by his squeals of delight that Justin remembered having seen the movie once before. At times he would smile appropriately as though he were listening to the conversation around him, so that day I was determined to reach him and find some way to allow him to communicate his needs other than crying.

However, my efforts were to no avail. The thought that perhaps he understood what I was saying and was just simply not trying hard enough to find some way to communicate was causing my frustration to morph into anger. I began angrily scolding him, and Justin began to whimper at my sharp tone. While anger and frustration were rolling off my tongue, Jennifer came up to Justin and gently touched his arm and said, "Justin, please try to do what Mama says; she just wants to know you love her."

It was as though her words flung open a shutter that had blinded my eyes to the motives of my heart. I thought I loved my children unconditionally, but even my four-year-old daughter knew differently. Their response to me, the measure by which they obeyed, was their payment for my love. This was one of those countless times during the years I cared for Justin that the Lord used him to open my eyes to the wretched condition of my own heart. I stood there silenced and dumfounded by the wise words of my preschool daughter. I realized I did not really understand unconditional love.

Unconditional love—it is almost synonymous with grace. This love without restraint, conditions, or limitations seems to go hand in hand with the unmerited favor of grace. That day I learned an important lesson: I couldn't offer what I didn't know I had, didn't know I needed, and wasn't thankful I had received. I couldn't offer unconditional love. All my love came with conditions. I lived as though God operated the same way. In many ways, my offering of love was my way of manipulating and controlling others—especially my children. I loved because they loved me in return.

Later that night, with a sorrowfully repentant heart, I knelt and asked for the gift of unconditional love. I wanted to be able to love my son unconditionally, and I knew I didn't. I thought I needed some great spiritual gift to give what I knew I couldn't, but in the midst of that prayer, I realized I had already received unconditional love. I had already been showered with grace in abundance. I had received it hundreds, thousands, millions of times . . . and I had received it once.

Christ died once for all my sin. He offered me unconditional love by dying so I could be saved by grace. He loved me so unconditionally that while I was a sinner—while I **am** a sinner—while I did and do love myself more than I love him, he gave his life for me. And it was that receiving of love—that receiving of grace—that finally overflowed out of my heart and toward my children.

Once more, my eyes opened to see myself in Justin. I was just as incapable of loving God or returning any good for the unconditional love and grace I was given as Justin. Recognizing the unconditional love, the grace, given to me moved my heart to extend kindness and love to my son. It didn't matter whether he could communicate and just wasn't, or whether he couldn't. I loved him anyway with a love that responded in kindness. I could love him unconditionally because I suddenly knew—really knew with my heart and not just my mind—that I was loved unconditionally.

☞ Chapter 29 ☜

Joyful Labor

*And people should eat and drink and enjoy the fruits
of their labor, for these are gifts from God.*
Ecclesiastes 3:13

While working for Paul, Robby and Paul had formed a partnership. They were farming a quarter section of land that had once belonged to Robby's grandparents and was now his parents' property. But disputes about how to split up the work were creating increased tension between Robby and the childhood friend who was now his boss.

By the time harvest was over and the holidays once more loomed ahead, the tension between Robby and his employer was so thick I was certain that Robby had already decided to quit at the end of the year. Neither of us knew what he would do to make a living for our family, but I knew Robby had always wanted to farm on his own, and I knew he was hoping the partnership he had started with Paul might give him a start in farming since the land they were farming together

219

belonged to Robby's family. Stepping out and farming on our own seemed very scary to me. I knew nothing about farm loans and business management nor did I feel I had the time or the desire to learn. A steady paycheck—even a small one—was a security to which I clung.

I felt as though I was holding my breath. I was waiting for the inevitable job loss while trying to survive a crumbling marriage and maintain enough control over my shaky emotions to care for Justin and manage our household. On top of all that loomed the added details and stress of a lawsuit. I was not surprised when Robby announced one evening, not long after Christmas, that he had quit his job and he had told Paul we would be out of the house in less than two weeks.

With another imminent move and the daily duties that consumed my time caring for my family and homeschooling the boys, I had little time to think about the lawsuit or to dwell on what the outcome could mean for our family, but Robby talked about it often. It gave him a hope that I could not seem to grasp. Knowing what had happened to Justin would set my mind at ease, but it would not change the outcome. And I could not fathom how a settlement would change the drudgery of the life to which Justin and I were bound. We discovered that since we had not pursued the suit early on, the statute of limitations had elapsed on the part of the suit that would allow Robby and me to sue for "pain and suffering" on our part. The suit had to be brought on behalf of Justin, and he would be the benefactor of any judgment. I was not disappointed by this discovery; I had a peace about the lawsuit and was content to leave the results in the Lord's hands. Life was simply too busy to dwell on it, and as the calendar heralded 1997, it looked as though it would be another year of change for our family.

With no job prospects in sight, my thoughts focused on where we would live, while Robby seemed to be as focused on the lawsuit as he was on a job. I knew our parents would do whatever they could to help us, but I still couldn't see any answers and I was not fully confident in my prayers. Though I prayed, I struggled to fully rest my confidence in God and completely trust in his providence. Justin's surgery had shaken my faith and my childhood belief that everything will always eventually turn out right, and although gratitude was slowly growing in my heart for the path that was now ours to travel, I had little faith for an uncertain tomorrow.

Robby talked of farming with his dad, but I was concerned that they did not have enough land to both support our family and provide for their own needs. However, Robby's dad decided to retire and let Robby take over his farm. Robby's parents found a farmhouse for us to rent nearby, paid a couple of months' rent, and we were soon somewhat settled in a new home. Only "somewhat" because the previous owner had passed away and her children had not finished sorting through the furnishings and belongings in the house. The garage and front room were closed off and filled with boxes and furniture.

However, we did not stay there long. Less than two months later, Robby's parents purchased another quarter section of land that included a beautiful old farmhouse. Of course, the farmhouse and surrounding property needed some work, but I loved the old homestead with its big trees and old barns. I had always longed for roots. I dreamed of someday owning a home where my children could grow up, a place where my grandchildren could return to play. I hoped this home would fulfill those dreams. Not long after we moved, the farmhouse where we lived while Robby worked for Paul was destroyed in a tornado, and so my prayers of thanksgiving for our new home were twofold.

Perhaps it was a sense of belonging that endeared me to that old farmhouse or perhaps it was because slowly—ever so slowly—I was beginning to see and believe that God was not only sovereign but he was also good. But for whatever reason, I loved that old farmhouse despite its need for some major repairs.

The seeds of thanksgiving and joy God had planted in my heart had sprouted, but it was there in that old farmhouse that those sprouts really began to bear fruit. As I began to see the depth of my sin mirrored in the way I handled my son, who could neither care for himself nor express any gratitude or love for me, I also began to see just a glimpse of my own brokenness and the depth of God's love for me. I had learned that without God's help to control my anger, I was incapable of remaining calm or offering any grace or compassion. My eyes were still slowly being opened to see myself in Justin. I was as incapable of loving God or returning any good for the grace I was given as Justin. Rather than unjustly punished, I was unjustly blessed—and that knowledge brought gratitude back into my heart. Once more I could praise God for my children—all my children. And as I began to thank him for my children, I also began to thank him for every other joy that came into my life.

So it was with deep gratitude rather than tears that I viewed the move into the old farmhouse. The house was not in any better shape than other houses into which I had moved with tears and dread, but a grateful heart helped blind my eyes to the faults and open them to beauty. Other old farmhouses where we had lived had also been surrounded with large old elms and barns, but I saw this home as beautiful and peaceful rather than old and in need of repair. Every morning through that first spring and summer, I would rise early and spend a few minutes with a cup of coffee in hand, walking around the old place praising God for the house and various little treasures I discovered as I walked. I prayed with my eyes wide open as though I were talking to a friend. Although the feeling that my world was void of God's presence still often plagued my heart, during those morning walks he seemed as close as a friend. The change to my heart was so gradual that it is difficult to pinpoint exactly when it began, but those early morning walks, those moments spent focused on praise, began to renew a joy I had resigned as lost forever, a joy that began to overflow into my relationship with my kids.

⌒

The first summer we were in the old homestead, Robby plowed and planted a large garden close to the house. He was excited about the prospect of selling produce at the local farmers' market. He also planted peas, cantaloupe, and watermelon at his parents' place. It soon became the responsibility of the boys and me to water, hoe, and care for the garden. The responsibility of a garden had been mine almost every summer since we were married, and I thoroughly enjoyed gardening, but past gardens were considerably smaller than our new one. The larger garden required much more time, so my mother began to come daily to help with Justin's care while the boys and I worked outside.

By this time, Jennifer, now five, was also a big help with

Justin. She often kept him entertained with movies and audio books while she played beside him. If he cried or became irritable or startled and had a seizure, she would come get me. Jennifer provided companionship for Justin now that I needed the boys to help more with the garden. Her help allowed me to work both inside and out without constantly checking on Justin or feeling as though I had left him unattended.

At my request, we added chickens and a couple of dairy goats to our growing farm. Since I grew up tending to chickens and helping with milking chores, I was excited to share the lessons and joys of raising farm animals with my children. The boys and I spent many hours working to repair old sheds and the barn. At first, our construction efforts were unskilled and left much to be desired, but we gradually improved. Although still very amateur, we did get better and were able to make functional improvements to the barn so it could accommodate our livestock and hay. Soon milking was part of our early morning routine. With Robby's help, we turned an old shed into a chicken coop; gathering fresh eggs also became a fun chore.

All the farm work, in addition to Justin's daily care and the usual responsibilities of raising a family, should have been daunting, but I enjoyed the labor. In the mornings while Justin slept, the boys and I would head to the barn before breakfast. While I milked, the boys fed the goats and chickens. The cool morning breeze usually carried the sweet smell of hay, and the swishing of milk in the pail sounded like music. Early morning walks and the time spent in the barn before breakfast were like a balm to my soul.

I loved working with my boys. Every project was an opportunity to spend long hours chatting while we worked.

Although there was a never-ending supply of projects, I tried to balance the work with plenty of playtime as often as I could. On warm summer days, after lunch the kids would play in the water while I finished Justin's lunch and cleaned up the kitchen. Then we would all gather in the cool living room to enjoy a good book together and rest.

As the summer days grew shorter and autumn approached, we were reaping a bountiful harvest, and the money we earned at the market made the extra work worth our efforts. The kids and I would pick the garden at the house every Tuesday and Friday morning. Then in the late afternoon, either my mother would come and help with Justin or we would leave him with my mother-in-law while the rest of us went with Robby to pick peas, cantaloupes, and watermelons. Those were long days and many times the sun was low on the horizon before we finished. As the sun set, I would pause to watch the glowing orb while the breeze rustled the dry leaves of the plants and the kids laughed and enjoyed a taste of a watermelon their daddy split open on the tailgate of the pickup, cutting out samples with his pocketknife.

Those moments were almost delightful were it not for the emptiness left by the one who was absent. My responsibilities to Justin weighed so heavily on my heart it was difficult to fully enjoy the moment. I felt guilty for imposing on the kindness and generosity of my mother, knowing she was handling the difficult task of feeding Justin and getting him ready for bed. Or I was anxious to get back to him if he was in the care of my mother-in-law because I knew it would take a while to feed and care for him, and the other kids also needed to eat and get in bed as quickly as possible. I wanted so much to enjoy those moments out in the field at the end of the day, but it was difficult knowing that caring for Justin when we returned home made the day even longer for my boys, who would often help with supper while I fed their brother. The long days were exhausting for Jacob and Jerrod, but despite their fatigue, they took turns rising early the next morning to go with Robby to take the produce to market.

After they left for market, the house was still and quiet while Jennifer, Justin, and whoever stayed home slept soundly. I took those opportunities to spend some extra time in Bible study and prayer. I felt as though I had never read my Bible before as I found something new in passage after passage. In addition to whatever passage I was reading, I also read a passage from Psalms, Proverbs, or Ecclesiastes. I read these three books over and over. I could not seem to get my fill of their words of prayer, praise, and instruction. They were food for my soul, and with them, my heart enlarged and overflowed with thanksgiving and joy.

⌒ Chapter 30 ⌒

Desperate Situations
and Miserable Mistakes

*Praise the Lord; praise God our savior! For each day he
carries us in his arms. Our God is a God who saves!
The Sovereign Lord rescues us from death.*
Psalm 68:19-20

With the added responsibilities of animals and a
market garden in the summer and educating Jacob, Jerrod,
and Jennifer the rest of the year, it was very difficult to keep
up with the hectic pace of the day and still rock Justin for
hours on sleepless nights, but somehow I managed to keep
that schedule. The new house had a second living area that
was far enough away from the bedrooms so as not to disturb
anyone with a light, so I no longer had to wrestle with Justin
or my own thoughts in the dark. I would often slip out of bed
and tiptoe to the den, where I could turn on a lamp and read
or write despite the weariness that weighed heavily on me.
Journaling, something I had done sporadically throughout
most of my life, once again provided an outlet for my

thoughts. However, chores at the barn, late night reading, and consistently early mornings kept me sleep deprived, and long hard days followed by long, sleepless nights are never a good combination for an extended length of time.

Justin still had a prescription for chloral hydrate, the sedative Dr. Linton had prescribed to use PRN, but I had started using it three or more times a week to help Justin sleep so I too could get some much needed rest. Even with the sedative, Justin would wake up once or twice every night, and I would reposition him and gently rock his waterbed until he relaxed once more in sleep. The sedative helped him go to sleep when it was time for bed and drift back to sleep if he awoke during the night. Without it, he continued to have bouts of restlessness and irritability that prevented him from sleeping, but I was uncertain whether it was safe to use it every night and I had not gathered the courage to call and ask Dr. Linton.

One night Justin was particularly irritable. Even after rocking him for some time after everyone else had gone to bed, I still could not get him to relax and go to sleep. I had given him the sedative just the night before and I was hesitant to give it to him two nights in a row. But it was already obvious he was not going to sleep any time soon. I was tired and ready to join the rest of my sleeping family, so I decided to give him a half dose. Two hours later, I was still rocking him. The sedative did not appear to have any effect on him, so I gave him just a little more—what I guessed to be about a fourth of a dose. Still it had no effect. I sat and rocked him in a hold that contorted my limbs but held his knees bent and his arms relaxed at the elbows and prevented his muscles from tightening. As long as I kept his body relaxed, he was quiet and dozed, but the second my muscles relaxed from fatigue, he would stiffen and once more start to cry. I thought back to the time, years earlier, when I had sat up with Justin and Jennifer for three nights in a row. I wondered why I didn't seem to have stamina to stay awake for just one night. My muscles were aching for relief and so, once more, I gave him what I guessed to be a fourth of a dose. Two more hours passed and Justin was still unable to relax and go to sleep, and I again gave him a little more of the medication. Still the medication continued to have no effect on Justin's stiff muscles and irritated nervous system. I administered a little more. In my sleep-deprived state, I tried to add up the number of small doses and remember exactly how much medication I had given. Suddenly I began to panic and worry that perhaps I had overdosed him. I had never given him that much before and the thought terrified me.

As the wee hours of the morning began to pass, Justin's tight muscles finally began to relax and give in to sleep, but fear overwhelmed me and I held him in my lap and monitored his steady breathing. I was afraid my weakness and selfish desire for sleep may have caused me to overdose my precious son . . . and I was scared. Overwhelmed with fear, I began to pray earnestly. I prayed for my son, for my own weakness, for forgiveness. And I prayed for wisdom.

Just as Jacob wrestled with God and held on tightly for a blessing, I wrestled with fear and frustration in those early morning hours of that long night, uncertain what to do. I prayed and wrestled for peace. I desperately wanted to know—not just hope—that God was really good and that he was there, ever-present in the circumstances of our lives. I needed to know that God was sovereign over our actions—

good or bad, intentional or unintentional—and that he was directing the course of our lives. But I was uncertain. I couldn't always feel God's presence, so how could I know that he was even concerned about my actions or their consequences?

In my own reasoning, I could conclude I was undeserving of mercy and grace and that any blessing or joy in my life came from God's goodness, but I wanted to know that every *struggle* also came from God's goodness—not his inattention. The night faded and the hours passed. I prayed and cried and prayed some more while Justin slept in my arms. As the light of predawn began to brighten the sky, Justin's sleep was deep and his breathing was steady and regular, but I was still afraid to put him in bed and afraid to sleep myself lest he lapse into a deeper sleep and stop breathing. I wanted to love Justin, but how could I love him through these moments? How could I care for him in these moments without losing my patience or overdosing him with a sedative in an effort to get him to sleep? And was God there—still present in our lives even when I stumbled and let selfish desires dictate my actions? Was God still sovereign and in control? Was God still good even when I wasn't?

While I wrestled with my guilt and begged for some sort of peace and understanding, I did not suddenly gain a deep understanding of theology, nor could I comprehend how God's sovereign will coincided with my sin. But somehow, I knew they overlapped and I was and had ever been in the hands of a sovereign God. I did not understand God's goodness in the tragedy in my life, but somehow I realized I could not and did not have to justify or define God's goodness in my life. God's nature was his and beyond my comprehension. It occurred to me as I sat there holding my son and praying that while I could not understand how a good God would allow me to suffer and allow Justin to suffer, my belief or unbelief in God's goodness did not change or alter God's nature. If God's nature did not change, and if God was good, he was good whether I believed it or not. And if God was sovereign, then he was sovereign even when I stumbled.

Just as I had once seen myself as handicapped in God's eyes and in desperate need of God's assistance to help me control my anger, I realized I could not understand, believe, or trust in his goodness without his help either. I once more saw myself as incapable of doing anything without his help—except sin. And although I was still responsible for my sin, I knew God was still sovereign and still good despite my sin. I knew I could not surrender my selfish desires by myself and I could not serve my son or anyone else without help. I also realized I would not have seen or recognized the depth of my selfishness were it not for desperate situations and miserable mistakes.

That night something in my heart grew a little more. Something changed a little more—what exactly, I still can't say, but I knew in my heart that God was removing a little more of the dross from my character, refining me just a little more. It was a process that would be repeated continually when I slipped and my brokenness revealed itself.

"Lord God," I prayed earnestly. "Please help me desire less of my will and more of you. Please give me the strength to put aside my selfish wants, even my need for rest and sleep. Help me to want more and more of you. Help me to be more like you and to serve my son with an unselfish love. I want to gladly surrender completely to your will—whatever it is—without resistance or complaint."

When the morning began to shoot rays of light over the horizon, I had an incredible peace knowing that God was good, sovereign, and in control despite my selfish and sinful actions. I knew that whatever happened, he was there. I knew he asked nothing of me that he didn't also supply. I may not have slept that night, but my spirit was renewed.

☞ Chapter 31 ☜

Happy Pills

I know, Lord, that our lives are not our own.
We are not able to plan our own course.
Jeremiah 10:23

One of my most dreaded tasks of Justin's medical care was the continuous paper trail that seemed to follow everything. Justin would qualify for home health or some other type of assistance; then programs would change and suddenly we would find ourselves without service. This was the case not long after we moved. The program providing Justin's respite care was changed, and we were once more without service. Although the service had always been sporadic because of the lack of qualified caregivers and my mother had graciously filled in many, many times, I desperately needed someone I could trust to keep Justin just a few hours each week so I could let the kids be involved in some activities provided by our homeschool group and I could run errands.

I applied for respite services through another program

called the CLASS program, but I soon discovered there was a long waiting list and it could be eighteen months before there was an opening. Since Justin received his therapy services through the school district, his therapy was not interrupted, but I dreaded taking him to town with me. His sensitivity to noise and overstimulation made a trip to the grocery store a difficult ordeal.

However, I devised a plan that my children would never forget. Once a week I would get up at 4:30 in the morning and leave for the store shortly after 5:00. Walmart was open twenty-four hours and our local grocery would open the doors a little before 7:00, so I could get all my shopping done and be back home by 8:30—just in time to get Justin up for breakfast. Every week I would take someone with me. Jacob, Jerrod, and Jennifer each took a turn getting up at 5:00, getting dressed, and going to town with Mom. It was a wonderful way to spend some time one-on-one with my children and they loved it. They called it "shopping in the night" because it was always dark when we left and often barely daylight when we got back. We usually finished up our trip with a quick stop at the Spudnut donut shop, which made the event even more of a treat.

I found myself thanking God for a difficult situation that forced me to find a creative solution and gave me some valuable time with each of my other children. It was a blessing to hear my children thank God in their prayers for our "shopping in the night" time together.

As the days grew cooler and our work in the garden began to diminish, our school days grew longer. We continued carrying produce to market until the first of October, which meant long days of picking at least twice a week. I felt we had gotten a late start on school and scheduled long school days to help make up for some of the time we had missed. Juggling school and a full therapy schedule for Justin had always been difficult, but as the boys grew older and Jennifer joined them, it became even more difficult. Music time, nature walks, and other fun activities that included Justin were no longer a daily occurrence. I did not want to exclude Justin from the quiet conversations, questions, and general activity of school, but I did not have the time to provide him with the rigorous therapy sessions we had done for years. Nor could Jerrod and Jennifer handle the distraction of therapy as I worked with Justin on standing and weight bearing, stretching, massaging his hands and fingers, auditory input, and my continual efforts to develop some sort of communication while they did their schoolwork. It was quite a dilemma.

About this same time, Justin's seizure activity began to increase once more. I knew that neither Justin nor I could tolerate the Ketogenic diet again, but his allergies to seizure medications limited our options. Once more, I found myself discussing our limited medication options with his neurologist. In the past, one of the few medications Justin tolerated well was Klonopin, but each time we discussed using it in addition to the Depakote he was already taking, I had opposed the idea because Klonopin was a muscle relaxer. It reduced Justin's tone and made it difficult for him to stand or step in his walker. But one day Justin's neurologist said something that made me seriously rethink my reasoning regarding Justin's daily therapy.

I had put my foot down once again on the Klonopin and he had concurred. "Of course, we don't want to take away any of the things he enjoys. If his walker allows him the freedom of mobility, we don't want to make him so sleepy that he misses out on his activities."

All the way home that day, I thought about the things Justin truly enjoyed: music, movies, and audio books. He also seemed content to sit and listen to us while we discussed various school topics and read aloud. However, he had never once attempted on his own accord to move any of his extremities to get something he wanted, nor did he give any indication that he wanted to be mobile. He thoroughly disliked both his stander and his walker because despite the high tone that made it possible for him to stand and bear weight, it was still a painful process for him. I was suddenly forced to really look at my motivation behind the rigid IEP schedule I had created for Justin and the intense therapy to which I subjected him—was it for his benefit or for mine? What did I really hope to accomplish with his therapy?

I knew the answer. I was still hoping that someday Justin would walk again . . . but in reality, that was unlikely. Justin still didn't even have good head control. He couldn't sit or push himself into a sitting position; he had gained none of the pre-requisite skills needed for walking even with a walker. His ability to bear his own weight on his legs could be an advantage in transferring him, but I rarely made him stand to assist in transfers. My mother and I had become very proficient at simply picking him up and carrying him. We both knew how to hold him and carry him in a way that was neither uncomfortable nor painful to him. Although I knew we might not always be able to transfer him by simply lifting him and carrying him, I also knew I had to reconsider Klonopin as an option for seizure control. And so soon after his eleventh birthday, I released my tight grip on his physical therapy, and we added Klonopin to his list of daily medications.

By the end of the first week, Justin's seizures were already better. His muscle tone had relaxed and I noticed he seemed more relaxed sitting in his little recliner. We had never used his wheelchair much at home, but he even seemed to tolerate sitting in his wheelchair better. However, the biggest change was in his demeanor. Within a week, Justin was calmer and happier. He smiled more, and he slept better. I don't know if he felt better or if it was a side effect of the medication, but life for Justin improved. I continued to use the chloral hydrate and after discussing it with Dr. Linton, we added it as a nightly medication. The combination of the chloral hydrate and the Klonopin made a major difference in his bedtime routine and greatly reduced the episodes of uncontrollable crying.

Fall passed and I missed our nature walks and watching the seasons turn. The garden and market kept us busy every minute we weren't working on school. There was no time for leisurely walks, but sometimes we took Justin's cart to the field and Jennifer, who was five, watched him and talked to him while the rest of us picked. The autumn afternoons were warm, but the searing heat of summer had passed and the dry leaves and ripe melons marked the passing of summer and beginning of fall.

After the addition of Klonopin, I no longer put Justin in his walker, and we soon stored it in a shed. A few years later, we donated it to Justin's medical supply company. I still scheduled time for Justin to stand in his stander most days, but long, busy school days with Jacob, Jerrod, and Jennifer often passed without ever getting Justin into the stander. Months had passed and we still had no caregiver, so I continued to do my grocery shopping once a week in the early morning hours before dawn. We either took Justin with us when we attended homeschool events since he was no longer quite as sensitive to overstimulation, or my mother would keep him.

The addition of the Klonopin was the final surrender of my overwhelming desire to control the outcome of Justin's life. As I surrendered Justin to God's hand, the anger that was killing me inside because I couldn't control him, couldn't control his cries, and couldn't reach past his brain injuries slowly burned out. I deeply feared that the awful feeling of helplessness fueling my terrible fire of anger would only be quenched by a drowning sorrow if I surrendered my desires to see him improve and to reach him and communicate with him. However, when I surrendered the preservation of my hope and dreams and gave up control, the peace-shattering, dream-crumbling anger subsided. I finally had the peace to love through each moment so I could live through each moment. I found myself enveloped with a peace that allowed me to embrace Justin with love regardless of what he did or didn't do.

≈ Chapter 32 ≈

Abundant Blessings

---

*He has sent me to tell those who mourn that the time of the
Lord's favor has come, and with it, the day of God's anger
against their enemies. To all who mourn in Israel, he will give a
crown of beauty for ashes, a joyous blessing instead of mourning,
festive praise instead of despair. In their righteousness,
they will be like great oaks that the Lord has
planted for his own glory.*
Isaiah 61:2-3

The first summer we sold vegetables at the market, we
were able to save enough money to purchase a new computer,
and a printer/scanner. This was a major purchase for our
family since a new computer and printer at that time cost
almost three thousand dollars. Robby was so encouraged
by our success that the following spring he acquired an
additional membership to the Lubbock Farmers' Market as
well as the Plainview Farmers' Market.

The Lubbock market was open on Tuesday, Thursday,

and Saturday and the Plainview market was open on Wednesday and Saturday. This meant we were picking almost every day of the week. Robby and one of the boys would get up early on Tuesday and Thursday to take produce to the market in Lubbock. The kids and I would take the produce to the Plainview market on Wednesday while Robby took care of his other crops. Saturday, Robby would take one of the boys with him to Lubbock and I would take everyone else with me to Plainview. Market became an all-consuming enterprise from spring until fall.

Every morning after Justin was fed and dressed and everyone had eaten, I would leave Justin in his recliner in the living room and ask Jennifer to entertain him while the boys and I picked the garden planted near the house. After lunch, everyone rested while I worked on laundry and other household duties. Then in the evenings, my mother would come to feed and bathe Justin while we picked the vegetables planted in the field. On Wednesday and Saturday mornings, whenever she was able, my mother came to stay with Justin and Jennifer while the boys and I carried the produce to market. Sometimes because of other commitments, she was not able to keep Justin and I would take everyone with me. It took everyone working as a team to run the table and keep Justin content. Thankfully, we were usually sold out by lunch and could go home before the heat of the day set in. Although the boys were just eight and nine years old, they worked long, hard hours in the garden and helped me keep the household running smoothly.

We were still without respite services, so I was grateful for the help my mother was willing to provide. I don't think I could have kept up with our garden chores without her. Her service was invaluable, though I found it difficult to accept her help because of the sacrifices I knew she made to give it.

In the middle of that busy summer, the first portion of our lawsuit was finally settled. Although the lawsuit was filed as one suit against the hospital and Justin's cardiologist, each case was settled separately. The suit against Justin's cardiologist was settled first. At the advice of our attorneys, we agreed to settle for the full amount allotted by her insurance coverage. Soon after the depositions were taken for this portion of the case, we learned from our lawyer that Justin's cardiologist was ill with breast cancer and her prognosis was not good. She was no longer practicing medicine, and her lawyer was doubtful she would even live to hear the results of the final settlement.

Although Justin's hospital chart for those first critical days following surgery was never fully recovered, depositions given by his surgeon and the nurses on duty at the time revealed even more than we suspected. It seems that Justin's cardiologist ordered Justin be given a controversial blood pressure medication the evening following surgery that— according to the testimony given by his surgeon—could have caused Justin to have a small stroke or minor brain injury that night. We knew the hospital was in the process of building a pediatric wing that would include a pediatric intensive care unit, but we didn't know most of the nurses in the ICU during Justin's stay were not trained in pediatrics and were not familiar with the differences in medications and procedures used with children. Nor did we understand how important it was that they have that knowledge. According to the testimony of other experts and those directly involved in his care at the time, the extensive brain damage Justin suffered was primarily a result of lack of oxygen during an improper procedure in which his cardiologist removed him from the ventilator without consulting his surgeon or pulmonologist. After removing him from the ventilator, Justin's oxygen levels recorded by a pulse-oxygen monitor began to drop, alerting the charge nurse in the intensive care unit. The charge nurse was assured by the cardiologist that a child could handle the lower oxygen levels but after almost forty minutes of extremely low oxygen levels decided to seek the assistance of an on-call anesthesiologist returning from the operating room. Before the anesthesiologist could convince the cardiologist to re-intubate him, Justin went into respiratory distress and was finally re-intubated by the anesthesiologist.

Even though I knew all the circumstances that contributed to Justin's brain injury and that his cardiologist had made some bad decisions regarding his care, I felt no anger toward her. I actually felt sorry for her family and for her little girl, who was not much older than Jennifer. I did not wish for her to suffer, and it troubled me that our lawsuit would cause her pain.

Most of the depositions for the suit against the hospital were taken at the same time witnesses were asked to give testimony for the suit against Justin's cardiologist, so Justin's surgeon and many of the nurses were only required to testify once. One surprising turn of events during depositions was the reaction from Justin's surgeon. We had not seen the surgeon since Justin left the ICU, and I wondered if he would even remember us since it had been over six years. However, he not only remembered, but he was also livid that nothing had yet been done to assist us. We discovered he went to the hospital board while Justin was in the ICU and reported what he felt was poor judgment on behalf of

Justin's cardiologist and the consequences. Our lawyer told us his actions probably flagged Justin's chart and caused it to be removed and reviewed by risk management long before I had ever requested to see it.

During the depositions, the attorney for the surgeon had to request a break for his client several times because the surgeon was so upset about Justin's current state and the fact that the hospital had never accepted the responsibility for the mistakes made in caring for him. It could be concluded from the depositions of experts and witnesses that Justin's brain injury was the result of a series of circumstances complicated by untrained and improper care and the poor judgment of his cardiologist. A few months later, the suit against the hospital was settled, and the hospital agreed to match the settlement made by Justin's cardiologist.

Finally knowing all the circumstances that led to Justin's brain injury did not change anything in our daily lives, but in my heart, it confirmed God's sovereignty. At any one point, the circumstances could have been altered and the results would have been different. If the medication given the night following surgery had been the only mishap in his care, Justin would have had a different life. Two nights later the surgeon had roused him and Justin was still responding to commands and slowly weaning off the ventilator. It was on the third day out that his cardiologist had prematurely removed him from the ventilator and caused Justin's extensive brain damage, but things might have been different if the charge nurse had sought assistance earlier. The hospital was willing and anxious to accept pediatric patients because they were training nurses to work in the pediatric ICU. However, it was not yet supplied well enough to provide services for pediatrics. And the hospital did not have a staff of trained pediatric nurses. Had we chosen to go to a pediatric hospital in a larger city, the care Justin received would have been different.

All these circumstances contributed to the devastating results of Justin's post-surgery care. Any number of changes to those circumstances would have created different outcomes, yet I had to trust that God was sovereign over the events of our lives. I had no emotional energy to waste on looking back and wondering "what if?"

Almost the entire amount of the first settlement was used to reimburse Medicaid for the additional medical expenses incurred because of Justin's brain injury. A small portion was set aside to open a special needs trust fund for Justin and to appoint a trustee. Robby and I had no direct access to Justin's trust, but we could request services and supplies, so our first request was that my mother be paid for the care she was already providing for Justin. After some negotiations, the board of trustees agreed. This was a tremendous relief to me because I did not like imposing on my mother's kindness. Unfortunately, it was fall before the agreement was final and the trust agreed to pay for fifteen to twenty hours a week of respite care. I was thankful for the arrangement, but I wished we could repay my mother for the help and countless hours she had sacrificed for us that summer. Now that she was his "official" caregiver, we simply kept the schedule we had established during the market season, and mother came every evening for two hours Monday through Friday to feed Justin and bathe him.

Once the final suit was settled, the lawyers paid, the money distributed to reimburse Medicaid, and the remaining put into the special needs trust for Justin, Robby and I met with Justin's trustee to discuss his needs. Our biggest need involved housing and a vehicle with a lift. The concern for the trust was, of course, the cost for such major purchases. Although the settlement was sufficient to cover Justin's past medical expenses with money left to invest toward Justin's future needs and expenses, the trustee wanted to guard against spending a large portion of the settlement. However, it was the opinion of Justin's court-appointed guardian ad litem that it was essential to make Justin's living environment disability friendly—just as important as his future financial security. Since the money was in a special needs trust, Justin still qualified for Medicaid; however, in the event of Justin's death, Medicaid would again be reimbursed for medical expenses with the funds remaining in the trust. It was with this knowledge that Justin's guardian ad litem strongly suggested to the trust company that our home and a vehicle be made top priority.

Since we didn't own our home, the first step would be to find out how much Robby's parents would want for the house and a few acres if we were to purchase it from them. The second step would be to get a few bids from contractors to figure out how much it would cost to make our current home accessible for Justin—including the addition of an accessible bathroom.

I loved the old farmhouse and hoped we could make improvements to it. However, after spending the summer looking for contractors and getting bids on the necessary improvements, it was the consensus of all the contractors that the old farmhouse needed some major work done to the foundation, a new septic system, and all new wiring. When all the bids were presented to the trust, the board of trustees determined it would be better to invest the money in a new home.

Where to build a new home became the next issue. Robby and I spent several months looking at land and calling landowners trying to find a place close enough to the farm and yet close enough to the highway that a gravel driveway could eventually connect to the highway and eliminate the concerns of living on a dirt road. At the same time, we were also looking at house plans and trying to determine what would best suit Justin as well as the rest of the family.

Robby bought a software program that would allow him to design floor plans and spent countless hours working on just the right design for our new home. He was very good at it, and the final design was a home that would accommodate all our needs for a long time. However, we still needed a place to build.

Meanwhile, we had also looked at several vans and lift options for Justin's wheelchair. We ran into an obstacle considering the amount of room needed for Justin's large, tilt-in-space wheelchair. A minivan would not work without removing both back seats, which would leave no seating for our other children, so that was not an option. A standard size van would leave a rear bench seat for all three kids, which would be acceptable, but did not allot for any additional passengers. That could become a problem within just a few short years as the boys and Jennifer outgrew the one-bench seat or we needed extra seating for a friend or two. In the end, we purchased a passenger van with a standard conversion package. The van was perfect for Justin because it not only had a lift to accommodate his wheelchair but it also had two rear bucket seats that reclined. This gave me a place to feed

Justin and a change of seating for him when daytrips took us away from home at lunch. This would help since Justin still did not tolerate his wheelchair for long stretches of time. It also had a rear bench seat that folded down into a bed. This gave me a place to attend to his incontinent needs since public restrooms were usually much too small. Even those that did accommodate his chair provided only a hard, cold floor on which to lay him. The van also gave us two extra seats for guests.

Since medication changes gave Justin more tolerance for outings, and the new van accommodated his needs, we were able to take Justin with us to homeschool events and other short trips. We became experts on roadside parks and parks in town because we packed a lunch every time we planned to be out during mealtime. Justin's diet of smooth, baby food textures, though not restrictive, required that I pack his food and his milk. It worked well to just pack a lunch for everyone and eat somewhere I could feed Justin in the van and then change him before we continued on our errands. I often expressed my sincere gratitude for the van that I felt the Lord had provided for us, but it was only one of many things for which I praised the Lord. As the years passed and my heart began to soften and fill with gratitude, I began to praise the Lord for many, many things that I thought others probably took for granted. I was surprised to find my own prayers of thanksgiving—though not always spoken aloud—reflected in the prayers of my children.

I listened as my six-year-old daughter said her bedtime prayer: "Dear Lord, thank you that I can see and that I know when someone is going to make a noise. Thank you that I can walk and I can tell Mama when I want something." Justin had lost so much, but his suffering made the rest of us extremely thankful for things we otherwise would have never given a second thought.

Because of Justin's auditory seizures, we were aware of every sound—every cabinet door or bathroom door that closed, every sneeze or cough, every click of a button or beep of an electronic device such as the microwave. We tried to anticipate every coming sound and forewarn Justin to help prevent an auditory seizure.

I was often amazed at the things my children noticed and the things for which they expressed gratitude in their prayers. Jacob prayed, "Dear Lord, thank you for people who make buildings without stairs and with ramps and thank you I can climb stairs and don't have to be in a wheelchair. Thank you that I can get out of the van and go in the store. Help Justin know we love him. Amen."

We knew every building and business that was not accessible. Even the hospital in Hale Center (which was an older building) was not wheelchair accessible from the front. Neither was our church. We became aware of how many people parked in the van- accessible spaces at major grocery stores, Walmart, and other places. We were always thoughtfully compassionate to those who truly needed those spaces and sometimes irritated with those who did not appear to need them as badly. More than once, my young children had to block traffic in a parking lot so I could back our van out of a parking space before letting the side lift down to either load or unload their brother. Going to town was, like every other daily function, a family effort, and my children became willing and loving servants to their brother. I thanked them and praised them often for their willingness to help. At night we would talk about how God was using their brother to build their character.

"I'm so glad we have Justin. Aren't you?" I would say as we were finishing our evening story time. "God uses Justin to help you learn how to help others."

"He uses Justin to help us know how to love others who can't talk," Jacob added.

"And if we didn't have Justin, we might not know how to do laundry or clean house because you might do it for us. Right, Mama?" Jerrod said as he restated one of the many ways in which his life was different from what it might have been if his brother were not handicapped.

Though at times they were disappointed when Justin's handicaps prevented them from participating in something, I never saw resentment in our other children. They graciously accepted the lot we had been given. I marveled at how quickly they could find the good in every situation and how grateful they were for simple pleasures. Their grace for their brother was truly humbling to witness, and it softened my heart toward Justin even more. I knew we had been blessed, and I was learning to be grateful. My children were learning to be grateful, and we all were discovering that a grateful heart is a contented one.

☞ Chapter 33 ☜

New Help

"For I know the plans I have for you," says the Lord.
"They are plans for good and not for disaster,
to give you a future and a hope."
Jeremiah 29:11

It had been a few months since the trust agreed to pay my mother to provide respite services for Justin. While we were still looking at housing and vehicle options, Justin's name and request for respite services finally made it to the top of the list for the CLASS program. He qualified for twenty hours of respite care a week.

Although I was glad we would once again be receiving services, I was skeptical about how long it would last and how consistent the care would be. We had been on a few other programs and had never received a caregiver who would stay for any length of time or could provide the quality of care I wanted for Justin. Either they were good but didn't stay long, or they were not willing to put in the effort that Justin's care required. I decided to request services for the morning hours and a longer block of time once a week that would allow us to run errands in town. I assumed mother would continue to come in the evenings, and I was more than pleased with that arrangement.

The help my mother provided was such a welcome relief. She came and stayed two hours every evening during the week. Many times, she came after working all day as a homehealth aide. I knew it was inconvenient for her and made her own evening routine late, but she came because she loved us and was willing to sacrifice her time as long as Justin needed the help. I was thankful the trust was able to pay her. Though I knew she did not do it for the money, I also knew she and my dad could use the extra income.

Once the market season was over and we no longer needed to work outside while she cared for Justin, our evenings became a time of pleasant fellowship for the kids and me, and we looked forward to the end of the day. Justin's new seizure medication and his nightly dose of choral-hydrate left him relaxed. While my mother cared for Justin, I was able to fix dinner and the kids could get their baths earlier. By the time she left, everyone was fed and bathed, Robby's supper was ready and waiting for when he came home, and Justin was calm and sleepy and ready for bed.

Robby didn't usually come in until after my mother left. I served him his supper, which he ate in front of the TV in the den. While I served Robby, the kids gathered in the living room with blankets and beanbags. Justin sat in his little recliner we had outfitted with caster wheels. One of the boys would push him into the living room. When everyone was ready, I would come and read aloud to them. Since our school days were longer, our afternoon reading times had all but disappeared, and the kids were excited that we could once more enjoy books together. It became a tradition that lasted long into their teen and young adult years, and we enjoyed hundreds of books together.

The first two caregivers hired by the homehealth agency for Justin's respite services funded by the CLASS program lasted less than two weeks each. Feeding Justin was still a difficult task—an acquired skilled that required patience to learn. As Justin grew older and heavier, carrying him and maneuvering him around in the small farmhouse bathroom without hitting his legs or feet against a doorframe were difficult. Lifting him in and out of the tub to bathe him was not a task for the weak or uncoordinated. Finding someone willing to take on the job and stick with it was not going to be easy.

In January, I received some standardized forms from Justin's trust asking us to update records on any changes in Justin's condition, his medication, any recent hospitalizations, and the services he was receiving. I hated all the paperwork still required for anything related to Justin's care, but I took care to fill it out diligently and listed the services he was now qualified to receive on the CLASS program. A few weeks later, I received a letter from the trust and was shocked and angered to learn they were no longer going to pay my mother for the respite services she provided because of Justin's new eligibility to receive respite from CLASS.

I wrote back and told them the homehealth agency through which we received the CLASS services was still unable to provide us with a qualified caregiver and that we had already tried two—neither of which stayed. Justin's trustee suggested my mother apply for the position and then she could be paid by the program for her services, but as I explained to the trustee, my mother was already employed by another homehealth agency. It would be a conflict of interest for her to be employed by both agencies. The trust was currently paying her as an independent contractor. After two months of correspondence, the trust finally agreed to once again pay my mother for the care she provided Justin since her assistance did not have any bearing on Justin's eligibility for the CLASS program.

While I was trying to get mother's respite services reestablished—of course, my mother continued to come and help care for Justin even when she wasn't being paid—a young mom named Stacy applied for the position offered through the CLASS program. She soon became the best caregiver we had ever had aside from my mother. She was very thin and I wondered about her ability to lift Justin, but Stacy quickly learned how to feed Justin, give him his meds, bathe him, and change him. She would come every morning to feed him, dress him, and get him ready for the day. My mother continued to bathe him in the evenings, so Stacy would work with Justin, stretching his legs, arms, hands, and feet and occasionally standing him in his stander. She would talk to Justin and my other kids while she worked, and I felt comfortable leaving Justin in her care while I ran errands in town or took the kids to activities and events sponsored by our homeschool group. With Stacy's help, our weekly early morning grocery runs were eventually replaced by a once-a-week afternoon trip while Stacy stayed with Justin for the entire day. She tended to his morning routine while the other kids and I worked on school lessons and sat with him in the afternoon while we were gone.

After feeding Justin almost every meal since he had his feeding tube removed five years earlier, I welcomed the help but was surprised to discover I missed feeding him. Justin was no longer a burden. It wasn't simply the additional help that eased my weary heart. I had let go of my expectations for Justin and was learning to simply enjoy him and every opportunity to serve him. No longer toiling for some distant goal and in the process wearing myself out both physically and emotionally, I was learning to be content with the child God had left me. When peace finally reigned in my heart, I was able to look on my child with love and mercy and find real joy in caring for him.

...down into a chair, ... one, and sat with him in the
darkness while we were gone.

✑ Chapter 34 ✎

Peace and Beauty

The Lord is my shepherd; I have all that I need.
He lets me rest in green meadows; he leads me beside
peaceful streams. He renews my strength.
Psalm 23: 1-2

By the time spring 1999 arrived, the lawsuit was behind
us. It was time once again to plant crops as another vegetable
market season would soon be underway. Robby once more
made plans to sell vegetables in both Lubbock and Plainview.
He and a friend also became involved in a test program
sponsored by Texas Tech University Ag Sciences. The
University provided us with four hundred tomato plants in
several varieties and provided soil testing for our garden plots;
in exchange, we agreed to keep records on how much each
variety produced, which meant we had to weigh each variety
after we picked it. Planting, picking, and keeping records on
four hundred tomato plants proved a major expansion to our
garden efforts.

As we enjoyed our new van and I was enjoying the additional help I was receiving from Stacy and my mother, Robby and I seized the season by continuing to look at land and consider our housing options. By the time summer arrived, almost a year after settling the lawsuit, we finally had a place on which to build a new home. Robby's parents had agreed to sell us four acres of land out of the acreage where we lived—actually they basically gave us the land since the exchange of such a minimal amount of money was only a formality. We chose a plot about two hundred yards off the highway, and the trust agreed to allow us to build there if the land was in our name and the house would eventually have access to the highway.

And so, in August 1999, a well was dug, the foundation poured, and our new home began to take shape. It was to our advantage that housing in our area was much less expensive than it was in the larger Texas cities and the trust agreed to the floor plan Robby designed when we were able to find a contractor who would build our home within the budget set by the trust. I had always been fond of the old farmhouse and was a bit discouraged to think our new home was being built right in the middle of a barren pasture, but I thanked the Lord for providing what he knew was best.

As the new house began to take shape, my heart continued its long process of surrender. I was gradually beginning to accept that Justin would—without a miracle—never walk, talk, or do anything independent again, but strangely, the letting go was not difficult; it was almost a relief. Justin still had physical therapy because I knew he needed to maintain the range of motion that he had in order for us to comfortably care for him. When a new school year began that fall, I requested only physical therapy from the school, and we met with no resistance. Speech therapy and occupational therapy became a thing of the past, and so our school day was only interrupted once a week now for outside therapy.

Justin's medications were finally such that seizure control was maintained at an acceptable level. He continued to have auditory-triggered seizures daily, but they were usually mild and were not followed by any additional seizure activity. Between the Klonopin and his nightly dose of chloral hydrate, Justin was not only sleeping better at night but he was also much happier and content during the day.

His cart continued to be the best means of transportation for him about the farm. Almost daily, the kids and I would walk down to check the progress on the new home and watch the builders from a safe distance. Gardening, canning, caring for a home, Justin, and homeschooling my children continued to keep me very busy. But sometimes while the sun was setting and the chaos of evening carried on inside, I slipped outside to enjoy the last rays of light, and my heart overflowed with gratitude for a few moments to enjoy the beauty of the sunset. These few seconds were always pure gold before heading back in to face wrapping up the evening chaos. Often in the evenings after my mother left, the children were in bed, and supper was cleared away, I would slip outside and soak in the quiet serenity of the autumn night and a more extended time alone. The quietness was calming to my soul, and I could once more find great joy in moments of beauty. A deep peace was growing in my heart and with it a deeper love and gratitude for my savior, who loved me despite my sin.

I had a deeper love for Justin too; I loved him regardless

of his handicaps and his inability to express love in return. Letting go of my expectations and simply accepting him as he was without any improvements was not something I could do on my own, but I accepted it as a gift—an answer to prayer. I no longer prayed that God would heal my son but simply trusted God to work out his will in Justin's life. That long night when I feared I had overdosed Justin was the last time I prayed for his healing. My prayers were now for my own healing—that God would heal me: heal my heart and give me the love and the strength I needed to love and care for my son. God was answering my prayer and giving me that love and strength, but what I didn't expect was the gift of gratitude and the deep joy that followed it.

As fall began to fade into the shorter days of winter, the farmer's market closed and the garden was plowed under for another season. The new house was now fully enclosed and continued to change daily. Winter and another holiday season approached, but the winter in my heart had passed and life was once more warm and joyful. I looked forward to the holidays with an anticipation I had not experienced in years.

However, when the day for our own little family celebration arrived, I was terribly sick with the flu. Despite a high fever, I forced myself out of bed to feed and tend to Justin since I had told Stacy she could have the week off for the holidays. I was thankful I had prepared enchiladas for our family meal in advance, but it was with disappointment that I served only the enchiladas without any side dishes. (Since two traditional turkey dinners usually awaited us at the extended family celebrations, we had decided to make it our own family tradition to have enchiladas, tamales, rice, beans, chips, hot sauce, and sopapillas as our Christmas meal.)

As I battled the flu, Christmas passed. Justin and I stayed home from family celebrations and passed the day listening to Christmas music and sleeping. The day after Christmas, Justin started running a fever and I began pushing extra fluids down him. The process was incredibly slow because he continued to have difficulty with thin liquids. I spent most of the day giving him small sips of water and other liquids to keep him hydrated. I knew the virus would be short-lived. I consoled myself with that knowledge, but for the first time since removing his feeding tube, I began to consider having it replaced. I knew a feeding tube would make feeding times much easier for both Justin and me, but I also knew that to go back to a feeding tube would in essence be admitting that Justin's feeding skills would probably never improve. Although I was beginning to let go of my own hopes and dreams for his improvement and my prayers had become requests for strength to cope with his restrictions, reinserting a feeding tube would be a major step backward, and it felt like admitting defeat.

Justin recovered from his bout with the flu as did each member of our family in turn, but I continued to consider the possibility of a feeding tube. A few weeks later, I made an appointment with Dr. Linton and discussed the idea with her.

"How is Justin today?" Dr. Linton spoke cheerfully as she entered the room. Though she always had a full patient schedule in addition to walk-ins she managed to squeeze in, she always made me feel as though she had all day and listened patiently to everything I had to say.

"Justin is doing well today," I said as she gently patted his arm while pulling the rolling stool up to sit down beside him.

As she sat down, I told her why we were there. "I brought

him in because I think maybe we should consider putting a feeding tube back in, and I wanted your opinion. Even though Justin has been without a feeding tube for several years, it's still very difficult to keep him hydrated. He hasn't digressed any, but I think his feeding skills may have reached a plateau, and it may be better if my mother and I weren't the only caregivers who could successfully feed him enough liquids."

She listened carefully and agreed. "If *you* think it's time to reinsert a feeding tube, then *I* think it's time to reinsert a feeding tube. I agree it's wise for you to have other options for those who aren't as skilled with his care. In the long run, it's much better for Justin." I nodded my agreement, and she added, "I'll be happy to set up an appointment with a gastroenterologist."

I thanked her as she left the room. A few minutes later, a nurse returned with the appointment information. I was surprised at how relieved I was to have Dr. Linton's approval and was anxious to get the procedure done so life could once more resume a normal routine.

Meanwhile, the work continued on the new house. As the house began to near completion, Robby and I did some of the finishing work to help save on cost. Robby laid laminate wood flooring in the kitchen and entry that to this day continues to be one of my favorite features of the house. At night after the kids were in bed and Robby was settled in front of the TV, I would go down to the house to paint the bedrooms and bathrooms. I did stencil ceiling borders in almost every room.

By late February 2000, the house was complete and I began moving a few things at a time. The kids were ecstatic about the new house. Jennifer and Justin each had their own bedrooms. Jacob and Jerrod shared a bedroom that had two closets, so they each had their own storage space. Justin's room and the master bedroom shared a bathroom that connected the two rooms. His room also had a ceiling lift that ran from his bedroom into a large walk-in shower in the bathroom. We ordered a large bath chair that fully reclined. We finally had an easy way to bathe him.

I loved the open space between the living, dining, and kitchen areas. However, I had been concerned that the TV would be a major distraction for the kids during school hours since much of their schoolwork was done in the kitchen, so we added to the floor plan a small den upstairs for Robby's TV room. We also put a small TV in Justin's room since movies were a source of great pleasure to him. We couldn't wait to get settled into our new home.

After our appointment with the gastroenterologist, Justin had a short-stay surgery to have his feeding tube reinserted in mid-February, but complications with the tube required it to be removed and a second tube reinserted. The second surgery was scheduled the first week of March—the week we had set aside to move—so while I stayed with Justin in the hospital, many of our extended family members came and helped move us into our new home. Justin and I returned to spend our first night home after the surgery in the new house.

☙ Chapter 35 ☚

Dark Days

---

*I can never escape from your Spirit! I can never get away
from your presence! If I go up to heaven, you are there;
if I go down to the grave, you are there.*
Psalm 139: 7-8

As spring approached, I was especially thankful for the
help mother and Stacy provided. Stacy continued to come
each morning to feed Justin and get him ready for the day.
She also stayed extra hours twice a week to allow me to run
errands or work outside in the garden, and mother came
every evening to help feed Justin supper and get him ready
for bed. The new feeding tube made mealtime much easier
for Justin's liquids, but we continued to feed him his oatmeal
and other soft foods by mouth since he seemed to enjoy them
and it made it easy to give him his seizure medication.

Once more, we planted a large garden including several
hundred tomato plants from Texas Tech that would require
extensive records. I thanked the Lord continually for the

extra help mother and Stacy provided so I could take on this task. After the garden was planted, my father came with his little tractor and helped the boys and me sod the backyard for several weeks while Robby planted his crops.

That summer, money was incredibly tight as the kids and I waited for Robby to apply for his farm loan. I was thankful for the income from the farmers' market, but it was not enough to provide for both our living and farm expenses, and I watched with dismay as Robby began to sleep less at night and spend more and more of his time during the day in front of the TV, computer, or napping and less and less of his time working. It appeared life had no meaning or purpose for him now that the lawsuit was settled and the new house was finished. He was irritable and restless and seemed discontent with all aspects of life. I had seen this pattern in him many times before, but I was determined not to let his attitude disrupt our household, so I inwardly withdrew from him even further. In the past, I had tried to encourage and defend him, but I never felt my efforts were successful. I had learned to shelter my heart by emotionally withdrawing from him. I had no experience with depression, and it wasn't until years later that I realized he was struggling with severe depression. I didn't understand why he couldn't rouse himself and get to work on the farm loan, so rather than feeling compassion for his suffering, my heart held only resentment.

Building the new house had given our marriage a temporary boost, but once we moved in, we were back on rocky ground. I continued to take my morning prayer walks whenever I could slip out of the house without angering Robby. He often wanted to sleep in and did not like anyone stirring—including me—before he was ready to get up. When

I had needed his help, he had not offered it, and in my pride, I had not asked. I had felt abandoned by my husband long before, left to myself to learn how to handle the emotional and physical aspects of Justin's care alone. I found incredible peace and joy in those quiet, early morning moments when I admired the beauty that seemed to be everywhere I looked and thanked God for countless blessings, but I did not share this time with my husband. I had found a joy that was no longer dependent on my relationship with my children or my husband. While I was able to share my happiness and delight with my children, I did not know how to share it with Robby. It saddened me that he did not see how desperately I needed those quiet moments spent in prayer. I had long ago given up the hope that he would join me in those morning walks, and the desire for his company had slowly disappeared. What I did not see was that perhaps now Robby was the one who felt abandoned and that the feeling of being left out was the source of some of his anger and resentment.

The constant schedule of people in and out of our house to assist with Justin was disruptive to the lifestyle Robby had grown up with and become he accustomed to. In the past, he had been able to set his own schedule based on the season, the weather, and how he felt without interference, and it angered him to have his household running on a set and unwavering schedule. However, looking back, I think his anger may have also been directed more toward the circumstances that had changed our lives than toward the interruptions that accentuated those changes. I should have understood since I too had struggled with anger. My anger had been unjustly directed toward Justin, but I felt Robby's anger was unjustly directed toward me. In my defense, I built an internal wall that blinded me to the source of his frustration and pain. I felt emotionally widowed. Rather than try to bridge the growing gap between us, I simply reciprocated his emotional withdrawal from our marriage. I had found peace in the circumstances of our life with Justin that Robby did not seem to share, and I could not help him.

Sometimes it seemed as though I was walking in the eye of a storm. While my marriage crumbled, I walked in silence, emotionally disconnected from my marriage, hurt and unable—or perhaps unwilling—to help Robby find the peace that now sustained me. My eyes were blinded to the confusion and hurt in his life. I had finally found peace from the emotional turmoil that had been my companion for years, so I watched in silence as our marriage crumbled, afraid to step into the whirlwind and offer any help to my husband in his struggles.

Robby finally applied for a loan in August. A month later we had money to pay off our maxed-out credit cards, but there was little left over for living expenses for the remainder of the year, and our crops were small. The atmosphere in our home was tense. As fall came, there was little to harvest. What should have been a joyous occasion as we celebrated the first Christmas in our new home was quiet and reserved. I seemed to have lost touch with my husband, and there was little conversation between him and the rest of the family.

I knew we had been drifting apart for years as I struggled with the responsibility of Justin's care as well as that of our other children and Robby struggled with the responsibility of providing for our family. We had divided the daily duties and responsibilities in our marriage long before Justin's surgery. In our youth, we did not recognize that our marriage was a covenant, and the duties and responsibilities of raising and providing for our family were ours to share.

I began fulfilling my heart's longing to love and be loved with a relationship with my children even to the extent of idolizing them, but I had not put the same effort into my relationship with my husband. No one had ever told us that we had to maintain our marriage just as we would maintain a hardworking tractor or our indispensable family van. Everything else seemed urgent, so everything else took precedence. We spent little time together, and the division in our duties created separate lives lived within the same walls. Adding to the divide, I was strongly influenced by our Christian curriculum and the homeschool friends and community with whom I fellowshipped, whereas Robby was strongly influenced by television. He held tightly to the worldview to which he was continually exposed.

Many farm wives work outside the home to help provide for the monthly expenses of the family, and Robby resented our family limitations and often expressed his desire for me to help with the income. He viewed our work in the garden and the money we earned at the farmers' markets as a compromise and a way I could take part of the responsibility for our family's provision without leaving home. I felt Justin's care kept me home, and his social security check was my contribution to our income. I had a strong conviction to homeschool our children, but I knew that were it not for the surprise blessing of Justin's handicaps that kept me at home and his social security check that helped with our monthly expenses, I would not be able to continue homeschooling. I just wished Robby shared my convictions rather than simply tolerating them. I wanted him to view Justin's handicaps as a blessing rather than a curse to our family. However, in my self-righteous pride, I could not step back and offer my husband any understanding, help, or space to grow and seek out his own answers, nor could I force him on a path that he refused to tread.

By spring, the tension in our marriage was intense. I had hoped spring might bring Robby renewed interest in life. It turned out that he had a few new ideas that seemed to give him a little energy and some hope that he could keep the farm and our family afloat. He ordered four hundred chicks and made plans to sell eggs along with the other produce at the farmers' markets as well as to health food stores. I was not excited about the chicks, and I feared they would be an added responsibility for the boys and me. The garden alone was more than I thought I could handle without taking advantage of Justin's caregivers—especially my mother. Our commitment to the farmers' market was just as hard on my mother as it was on the kids and me. She often went above and beyond her duties to Justin to help me with his care so I could do the work required to tend, pick, and sell produce.

While Robby viewed the garden and market work as my job and thought I should be grateful for any help he gave, I viewed it as an extension of his job and thought he should be grateful for any help we could offer. I felt it was unfair for Robby to expect the boys and me to work so hard to help provide the income our family needed, and I had little compassion for the burden he carried. I felt Robby still selfishly wanted things to be as they might have been if Justin had never had a brain injury and that he was privileged to be able to ignore the hardships of Justin's care. I never considered that perhaps he was still struggling with the reality of Justin's handicaps.

There were other issues besides those major battles over the market and our finances. Looking back, it is difficult to say what the final turning point was, but by May our marriage had reached a crisis. On May 16, 2001, I filed for divorce. I did not want to destroy my husband either financially or emotionally; I just wanted a reprieve from the work and the emotional strain of our crumbling relationship. But on May 18, 2001, our world was shaken to the core when Robby took his own life.

The next several days were a blur. His family blamed me and I blamed myself—it was my decision to leave that seemed to be the final blow, more than Robby could handle. I struggled to make sense of anything as my own shock had yet to fully set in. The kids were scared, confused, and in shock. Robby's family directed their hurt and anger at me. His parents made all the funeral arrangements, which proved to be a blessing since I had no idea what to do and was having a hard time even thinking clearly.

I was just trying to hold our family together and I had no idea how to reconcile my relationship with the Campbells. The kids and I were just thankful to be included with the family at the last minute on the day of the funeral. Jennifer was eight, Jerrod eleven, Jacob twelve, and Justin fourteen. And suddenly, they were without a father.

The tragedy of that day left me once more feeling as though God was absent from my life. There were those who continually reassured me that it wasn't my fault. But although I did not admit it, my conscience still plagued me. However, one lesson I had learned through those trials and long nights wrestling with Justin was that although I am fully responsible for my sin and the decisions I make and must live with the consequences of those decisions, God is still fully sovereign—even over my sin. And I knew in my heart that if God is sovereign over sin, he is sovereign over life and death. I longed for the comfort of his peace and the feeling of his presence. Even though I could not feel him, I knew his grace was sufficient and I clung to that assurance. I was reminded of the night I feared I had overdosed Justin and how my selfishness could have had unintentional but devastating consequences. It didn't and Justin was fine, but I somehow knew then that God was sovereign.

This time everything was not fine, and my heart was once more broken by my own selfish desires and the unintentional consequences of my actions. I knew that this horrific tragedy was not the result of my decisions alone and that I had no power over Robby's actions. I realized he had likely already given suicide a good deal of thought since he had acted so swiftly, and yet I knew that our sins—like all things in marriage—were entwined. I felt as though I had wandered from God, seeking my own solutions to the overwhelming problems of our marriage. But I took comfort in knowing my will does not hold me close to the Lord—rather it is his hand that always draws me near.

In the days and months that followed, my heart in hurt and confusion cried out to my Lord and my prayers whispered, "Why?" Then I would be reminded of C.S. Lewis's story *The Horse and His Boy* in which Aslan, the great Lion, the son of the Emperor-Over-the-Sea, the King above all High Kings in Narnia says to the boy Shasta, "I tell no one any story but his own."

I will never know or completely understand Robby's story. I only know my own story—his is not mine to know.

I often remind myself that it's not necessary to untangle the web of destruction that led to Robby's death and to determine who was responsible for each part, but that God's grace is sufficient to cover it all.

~ Chapter 36 ~

Adjusting to Change

Don't worry about anything; instead, pray about everything.
Tell God what you need, and thank him for all he has done.
Then you will experience God's peace, which exceeds anything
we can understand. His peace will guard your hearts and
minds as you live in Christ Jesus.
Philippians 4:6-7

Two weeks after Robby's death, our homeschool group changed the venue for the annual end-of-school party—everyone met at our house for a workday. All the men pitched in to build a half-acre pen for our goats and helped relocate the chicken pen. I felt as if their kindness and help came directly from God's hand—and it did. I was not abandoned; I was forgiven and covered by grace.

The rest of the summer passed in a blur. A market garden had already been planted. I felt it would be a waste if we didn't at least attempt to take some of it to market, so the kids and I continued to sell produce at the Plainview market that summer. I knew we couldn't keep up the demands of two markets, move the remaining livestock and hay in the barn, sort through the things stored in the outbuildings at the old farmhouse, and get our farm equipment ready to sell as well, so I canceled our membership to the Lubbock market.

We worked hard that summer. The hard work seemed to keep my mind so occupied that I could not think about what happened. It was a convenient distraction from my grief. By the end of the summer, we had moved all our remaining belongings from the old farmhouse. It was with a deep sadness that I walked through the old barn for the last time. I loved the old pole barn with its big high rafters and sloped sheds on each side. My favorite little milking room was set at the end of the long shed on the east side of the barn, and I lingered there a moment, wishing circumstances could be different. There was a nostalgic air to the old barn that made me feel as though I had stepped back a hundred years in time. Although I had plans to build a new barn, I knew it would never look or feel the same as that old one we were leaving behind. Milking, caring for kids (goat kids), and the other responsibilities that forced me outside each morning and evening had given me permission to step into a place that calmed and relaxed my spirit. It was more than just the goats and the gentle rhythm of milking that had a calming effect on my heart—it was the very atmosphere of the old barn. I knew I would miss it. I would always look back on that place with fond memories because it was there that the Lord taught me to still my heart. It was there that he gave me the strength I needed to deal with the daily demands of Justin's handicaps. It was in that house and barn that my anger toward Justin was finally quieted. And it was there that the Lord slowly replaced anger with tenderness and love. True, new medications had improved Justin's temperament. The help I received from my mother and Stacy had helped lighten the load I had carried for so long, but the Lord had also changed my heart and it was here that I found true peace and joy.

I knew these gifts I gained while living in that old farmhouse came from the Lord and were not connected to the house or the place, but it was with a heavy heart that I took one long last look around the old barn and farmhouse. As I walked down the path that led to our new house, I prayed that the Lord would fill our new home with peace—a peace that would be evident to all who entered its doors. As I prayed, the Lord filled my heart with an inner calm.

What I knew in my mind connected with my heart. Peace and joy are not contingent on a place or time. They are a gift that can be opened wherever there are hearts that need healing.

Earlier that spring before Robby's death, Stacy had announced she was expecting another baby. We were excited for her, but I also knew she would have to quit before the baby arrived. After Robby's death, she agreed to stay until August, if possible, to help through as much of the market season as she could and to give us time to get things moved from the old house and ready for a farm sell.

Robby's brother and my nephew worked hard that summer to help us get farm equipment ready to sell. By late August, the farm equipment sold and I had set up an estate account with the help of my lawyer to distribute the income toward the farm debts we had accumulated.

Stacy left in August and we quit taking produce to market in early September. My mother continued to help us in the evening, but after three failed attempts to find a reliable caregiver to replace Stacy, I decided I would just care for Justin myself in the mornings.

That fall, Justin was fitted for a new wheelchair. The new chair had a thick foam seat and back. It had cushioned side supports and cushioned armrests—unlike the bar armrests on both of his previous chairs. A fitted headrest cradled his head and a stretch elastic band prevented his high tone from pulling his head forward. The elastic band was designed to move side to side with his head movements. For the first time, Justin had a wheelchair he could tolerate sitting in for several hours at a time. The new chair quickly replaced his little recliner (which he was outgrowing) as a feeding chair. He no longer spent time lounging in the larger recliner but was able to sit in his wheelchair for long periods without being repositioned. He was also outgrowing the cart we had used for so many years to transport him about the farm, but the large wraparound porch and cement ramps gave his wheelchair access to the outdoors.

Life without Robby was different, and yet strangely the same. I had not realized how much our family had divided. By the time fall arrived and the farm sell was over, we quickly adjusted to a routine of work, school, and therapy that differed little from that of previous years.

Then on September 11, 2001—just four months after Robby's death—the terrorist attack on the twin towers occurred, and the news left me feeling vulnerable and alone.

It was the first time since Robby's death I had even felt lonely, and that left me struggling with guilt.

Several weeks later as I watched the cotton harvest from our upstairs window one night, I realized how much I missed Robby—I had missed him for years. I missed spending time with him in the field even when I had three little boys in tow; I missed talking in the evenings after kids were in bed and the kitchen was clean; and I missed attending church and family functions together as a family. There were many things I had missed for years. Our marriage, like our sinful hearts, was flawed with cracks in its foundation. The hardships of Justin's handicaps revealed the personal flaws in each of us and opened deep cracks in our marriage.

I had wanted Robby to help me learn to care for Justin. I had wanted him to help me as I struggled to understand and accept what had happened to our beautiful little boy. I had been too prideful to ask for help and hurt that he had not noticed how much I needed him. Robby's emotional absence had forced me to shift my dependence onto the only one who could ever really offer the help my heart needed. Instead of trusting in a man, I was forced to see my need for a savior. Although I would have preferred to learn that truth another way and I wish we could have mended our hearts and our marriage, I was still grateful for hard lessons learned and a heart that was beginning to mend.

Robby had two life insurance policies when he died. Because both policies were several years old, they paid within a month of his death. Neither policy was tremendously large, but they provided the immediate income we needed while I applied and waited for our social security survivor's income. However, one negative effect of the insurance money was that it disqualified Justin for his disability income and Medicaid benefits. So for two months while we waited for his survivor's benefits to become effective, he was without Medicaid. I was thankful for the trust that paid both Stacy and my mother during that time in addition to covering Justin's prescription medications.

When the men in our homeschool group built the fence to contain our goats, we moved all the animals from the old barn. However, they were without a shed and we did not have a place to store hay and feed. I had actually enjoyed milking outside throughout the summer and into the fall, but as the days grew shorter, I no longer watched the sun rise and set as I milked. Now that I milked in the twilight before dawn and after dark, I knew we would soon need a barn.

It felt strange to plan the construction of a barn without Robby. I struggled with making the final decisions and found myself second-guessing every choice. Finally, I did call and arrange to have the foundation poured for the barn and a back patio poured. Justin was quickly outgrowing his cart, and I knew he would soon be confined to his wheelchair and to the porch. We also poured a sidewalk that connected the patio to the cement slab in front of the garage. This allowed Justin to be easily transported from the front porch, down the ramp, around the garage, and down the sidewalk to the back patio. We could use the ramp off the back porch to reenter the house or go back around to the front. It was not as much freedom as the cart allowed, but it did allow him to be outdoors while we worked in the yard.

The winter after we moved, natural gas prices soared. Our income was extremely tight, so Robby had purchased a chainsaw to cut our own firewood, and we began to burn firewood to help heat the house. The fireplace was designed so we could either burn wood or use a gas insert so it could function as a natural gas heater. It had an electric blower that made the fireplace much more efficient than a traditional wood-burning, open-flame fireplace. That fall after Robby's death, I learned to operate the chainsaw so we could continue to cut our own firewood and help reduce our heating expenses, thereby stretching our social security income.

When mother came in the evenings to help with Justin, the kids and I loaded into the pickup and drove up to a grove of old elm and mulberry trees on the far side of the farm to cut down dead wood. The boys quickly became skilled with an axe and could split the logs almost as fast as I could cut them. Jennifer gathered smaller sticks for kindling. When we were done, everyone helped load the pickup. By the end of November, we had several cords of wood stacked for the winter.

I had asked a friend who was in construction to build the new barn, and by Christmas it was finished. A more modern structure with a concrete floor, it held little resemblance to the old pole barn with its dirt floors, but it was nice and easily suited our needs. It also had water and electricity so I no longer milked in the dark.

As Christmas approached, the kids and I had several discussions about our holiday traditions. Life was changing for everyone, and our three-day holiday marathon was changing. Although we were still invited to spend Christmas Eve with my in-laws, the day would be different without Robby. Other changes were occurring in the Campbell family as well. Grandchildren were growing up and leaving home, and it was evident that family traditions would begin to adjust as children grew up and families changed.

Traditions were changing for my parents as well. That year they decided to travel to New Mexico to spend Christmas day with my brother, who had moved in recent years. Since it would be difficult for us to travel with Justin, they were planning on having Christmas breakfast with us before they left. This meant that for the first time since I had left home, our family would not be spending Christmas day at my parents' home.

One evening before the holidays, I gathered my children together to discuss the changes. "This year Nana and Papa are going to come and eat a nice Christmas breakfast with us on Christmas day. Then they are going to New Mexico see your Uncle Michael and his family and eat Christmas dinner with them." The fire crackled and cast a warm glow into the room. Justin appeared to doze in his chair, and Jacob stared into the fire thoughtfully while Jerrod and Jennifer warmed their backs beside me by the fire. I continued, "We will be going to Mamma and Grandpa's on Christmas Eve as usual, but I was wondering if you would like to celebrate our family Christmas on Christmas day after Nana and Papa leave."

Jacob spoke first. "I don't really want to change anything about our Christmas. I think we should still have Christmas on the day before Mamma's."

Jerrod and Jennifer nodded their heads in agreement, and Jerrod added, "I don't want to wait until Christmas day; I want to have our Christmas first just like we always do."

"Okay then. We'll have Christmas on December twenty-third," I said cheerfully. I paused for a moment before I continued. Earlier that day I had confided to a friend that I dreaded decorating the house for Christmas and seeing all the things that might remind us of Robby—especially our monogrammed stockings. Her children were older, and she had shared with me one of her family traditions. Now I was anxious to suggest it to my children.

"What if we change something about our Christmas? Maybe start a new Christmas tradition?" I asked. No one spoke, but they were all listening attentively. "What if instead of hanging stockings, we set out a gift bag for everyone; you can all pick out your own decorated bag. Then everyone can buy a few small gifts to go into the bags—things like you might get in your stocking. You can put the gifts in the bags early if you want to and look at them, but you can't take them out or open anything until we have our Christmas on December twenty-third. Then we can try to guess who gave us what as we open them."

I held my breath as I waited for their response. Thankfully, they were excited about the plan and eagerly agreed. So Christmas once more arrived early at our house just as it had for years. Our gift bags sat on a small, decorated table in the living room. For two weeks before Christmas, everyone participated in filling the bags by slipping in small gifts at random. The kids had a lot of fun making and buying small, inexpensive items and then trying to slip them into the bags unnoticed. They also had fun guessing who had put each item in their bags. By December 23, every bag was filled to overflowing with small gifts. The absence of their father was still felt keenly by all, but opening the small gifts that filled the bags and symbolized the love we shared for each other helped ease the loss felt on that first Christmas after Robby's death and became a longstanding tradition.

⌒ Chapter 37 ⌒

Life Lessons Continue

Those who live only to satisfy their own sinful nature will harvest decay and death from that sinful nature. But those who live to please the Spirit will harvest everlasting life from the Spirit. So let's not get tired of doing what is good. At just the right time we will reap a harvest of blessing if we don't give up. Therefore, whenever we have the opportunity, we should do good to everyone—especially to those in the family of faith.
Galatians 6:8-10

On December 26, the snow began to fall. Within the next twenty-four hours, we received several inches. The first days of the snow were joyous. The hazy winter sky and the snow-covered yard were beautiful, and being snowed in gave us some much needed family time. No one—including my mother—was able to get to the house. Even after the snow melted, it would be several days before the road dried out enough to be passable since the only road to the house was dirt. The gravel drive running to the highway was still just a plan.

It had been a very hectic and busy fall season, and I felt we needed some leisure time, so school was out for the week. But several leisurely vacation days soon had my heart once more focused on self, and I needed a reminder about faithfulness, strength, and joy. Although we were enjoying the break from our routine schedule, several days without any help was beginning to wear on me. Justin now weighted over 120 pounds. Though we did use his wheelchair more, we rarely used his ceiling lift, and I still just transferred him to and from his chair by picking him up.

I was finishing his lunch after everyone else had already left the table. In the middle of his meal, it became obvious he needed to get out of his wheelchair for a few minutes. "Oh, Justin, not now," I groaned. For a moment, I was angry with him although he was not at fault. "Now it will take me twenty minutes longer to finish lunch," I thought as I pushed the wheelchair toward the bedroom. "Plus two more transfers on my back," I selfishly added.

Suddenly the scripture came to my mind, "Be not weary in well doing." The thought sharply admonished my soul. "Oh Father," I prayed, "forgive me for my selfishness."

The time was unimportant; I simply wanted a nap. I realized I was seeking my own solution to my weariness—both mental and physical. I had forgotten the true source of my strength, and that was once more robbing me of the joy of caring for my son. I found myself reminded of the blessings Justin had brought to my life, and I realized that serving him was no longer an obligation—it truly was a blessing. As an obligation, it had been a duty to care for him. But seeing his handicaps as a gift had opened my eyes and continued to open my eyes to the true condition of my heart. I began to view every moment spent caring for him as a labor of love.

We made it past the holidays that year without the usual winter colds, but by early January, several of us had the sniffles. What appeared to be just a simple cold for everyone else hit Justin especially hard. He had not been sick long before I decided to take him in to see Dr. Linton and get him something to help combat what I thought was probably bronchitis.

However, as soon as Dr. Linton saw him she noticed that he was breathing heavily, and she immediately hospitalized him with pneumonia. While in the hospital, Justin had some chest x-rays followed by an echocardiogram. The tests revealed what I think Dr. Linton suspected—Justin was suffering from congestive heart failure. His heart valve was no longer functioning as it should, and his enlarged heart was suffering from increased strain due to the weight of his upper body and a lack of upper-body strength. Surgery was not an option I would consider, and no one pressured me to give it much thought. His seizures alone were a complication that would make surgery risky. I decided to have a cardiologist simply monitor his condition. I was told that many people live with congestive heart failure for years, so I tried not to dwell on the diagnosis.

Justin spent the next several days in the hospital. The kids, now ages nine, twelve, and thirteen, stayed at home with grandparents stopping by to check on them frequently and my mother staying with them at night. This made it much easier for them to care for the animals, as they were quite capable of handling all of the daily chores without my assistance.

Within a few days, the fluid in Justin's lungs had

diminished, and he was beginning to have a productive cough. I was hopeful we would soon be returning home. Caring for Justin in the hospital was far more difficult than it was to care for him at home. Just finding space in the hospital room to maneuver his wheelchair into a position that would make feeding him manageable was next to impossible—and then I had to get him to eat! He simply didn't like hospital food. Also, it was usually much easier to bring his meds from home rather than depend on them to be delivered to his room according to the med schedule we maintained at home. G-tube supplies and incontinent supplies for a child his size—not a small child and yet not an adult—were usually in short supply, and a bed bath was our only option for bathing. I was thankful when we were finally able to return home.

Because his 02 stats were still low—especially while he was sleeping—an oxygen concentrator was prescribed for Justin and he began to sleep with an oxygen cannula in place at night. Dr. Linton also prescribed a new nebulizer and medication so we could administer breathing treatments at home as needed.

Just a month after Justin was released from the hospital, I got a phone call from my friend Janet Norton. The Nortons had moved from Amarillo to Winters, Texas, the previous year. Although we seldom saw each other as we once had when their family would stop by and visit after Janell's doctor appointments in Lubbock, we had stayed in touch. I knew something was wrong by the tone of her voice when I answered the phone. "Hello, Sheila, this is Janet." Her voice wavered.

"Hi, Janet. So good to hear from you. Is everything okay?" I asked.

"Our precious Janell has gone home to be with the Lord," she said as her voice broke.

I waited for a few minutes as an incredible sadness passed over me. Then I answered softly, "I'm so sorry. When?"

Although we knew children with cerebral palsy can and do live into their thirties or even longer, we also knew that they were very susceptible to fatal complications from the various medical problems that often accompany cerebral palsy. Many do not live into adulthood. We had talked about the possibility of losing our children before, but the finality of those words struck me hard. Janet went on to share the details of her passing and gave me the information about her memorial service. She did not expect us to come but simply wanted us to know. However, I was determined to go and support my friend and her family if at all possible. The Nortons had been such good friends and had supported me at a time when I desperately needed it. Now it was my turn.

The day of Janell's funeral was bitterly cold. My mother agreed to spend the day with Justin while we drove three hours to Winters to attend the funeral. It was the longest road trip my children could remember taking. Were it not for the circumstances, we would have enjoyed traveling together. We arrived just in time for the graveside services, which were held before the memorial service. It was nice to see Janet and her family, but I wished that it had been under better circumstances.

As spring began to once more unfold and the days grew longer and warmer, we discovered our new back patio was a terrific place to eat, and it gave Justin better access to the great outdoors. Since the patio was poured late in the fall, we had not used it much before colder weather forced us indoors. In the evenings after my mother left and everyone was ready for bed, we would sit outside and I would read aloud.

Planting a large garden to raise produce for the farmers' markets had become almost second nature to us. We found it surprisingly difficult to reduce our garden now that we weren't selling produce. Once more, we prepared the half-acre patch behind our new home. I purchased fifty tomato plants, which did not seem like many compared to the four hundred plants we had put in the year before. But by the end of the summer, we had far more tomatoes than we could use or can. Since we no longer had access to irrigated rows on the edge of the field crops to plant peas, cantaloupe, and watermelon as we had in the past, those crops were also planted in our half-acre plot. It was a major relief to finish picking the garden in only a few hours. When fall came, we plowed the garden under with tomatoes still on the vine. I had no regrets.

That summer the kids used some of their own money they had saved to purchase an above ground swimming pool. In the late afternoons, they swam while Justin and I sat on the back porch and enjoyed listening to an audio book or music. It felt good to see them enjoying their summer. I realized that just as I had pushed Justin to improve by providing him with continual therapy even when it proved to be painful and delivered minimal results, we had also pushed the other children—especially Jacob and Jerrod—to become young adults while they were still boys. We had started selling produce at the farmers' market when they were only seven and eight years old. What had started as a way to simply earn extra income had quickly become a way to earn a large portion of our living expenses. Now they were twelve and thirteen and I wanted them to enjoy childhood and summer before they both passed.

However, the boys were accustomed to hard work. That summer they decided to build a clubhouse using the lumber from an old deck we had disassembled and the lumber from an old clubhouse their dad had built when they were younger.

I agreed to the project, but was quite shocked as I watched it progress. The finished product was a six-by-six clubhouse with a four-by-six deck atop a lattice-covered gazebo and a small storage room. They added to the old deck stairs to create a staircase running along the outside of the structure with a small landing. A second flight led to the deck above. The clubhouse had a door, a pitched roof with shingles, and windows with plywood shutters. They built bunk beds in the clubhouse. With the help of a friend who was an electrician, they wired it for electricity. They added lights and a small portable fridge that we had used for market and often carried a small TV and VCR outside to watch movies. They spent many summer nights sleeping outside and watching movies in their new structure. It was nice to see them enjoying summer and enjoying life.

As I continued letting go of my expectations for Justin and holding fast to my love for him—a love without expectation—I was also learning to let go of the expectations I had unintentionally placed on my other children. Just as I had begun to praise the Lord for everything I could possibly find good in Justin's circumstances, I began to praise the Lord for my other children. I asked God to help me not expect adult work from them. It was difficult because there was still a lot of work to do. We built and repaired sheds and pens for the goats and chickens, we cut our own firewood, and we planted grass and trees in our large yard. The clubhouse was also evidence of their abilities despite their age, but I prayed the Lord would help me break my habit of expectation. I wanted to enjoy my children—all of them—for who they were and not for what they did or didn't do.

☞ Chapter 38 ☜

Difficult Decisions

Trust in the Lord with all your heart; do not depend on your own understanding. Seek his will in all you do and he will show you which path to take.
Proverbs 3:5-6 NKJV

September 11, 2002. As our nation mourned the anniversary of that dreadful terrorist attack that had become known as simply 9–11, our family enjoyed the beauty of autumn without the stress of garden work. There was still firewood to gather for winter, so once again, we cut wood from the small patch of elm trees located on the far side of the farm. We went in the evenings while Nana fed Justin his supper. Although collecting enough firewood for winter was a major chore, we still made time to enjoy the cooler weather and the changing seasons. Since we could no longer take Justin with us as we walked and explored nature, we put up several bird feeders around the house and took time to be still and watch as the season changed around us.

In the evenings as the shorter days hastened the sunset, the boys would start a fire in a small barrel beside the back patio. We spent many long evenings sitting outside long after dark enjoying the warmth of the fire against the chill of autumn and the warm fellowship of each other's company. Once Justin was fed and ready for bed, we would wrap a blanket around him and put him in his chair so he could join us on the patio after Nana left. My heart was finally quiet. I had an inner calm that reflected the tranquility of those peaceful evenings. As I often recorded in my journal, I was blessed beyond measure.

While the autumn days grew shorter and the holidays approached, Justin was once more hospitalized with pneumonia when a cold quickly settled in his lungs. This time when he came home, we added a new medication to his growing list of meds—the diuretic Lasix sometimes known as Furosemide. We all got flu shots that year to help prevent Justin from being exposed to anything more serious than a cold, and I began to realize how fragile he had become. It surprised me because the steroids he had been on multiple times had given him the appearance of being thick and healthy. I had not realized that his brain damage and subsequent handicaps would have such

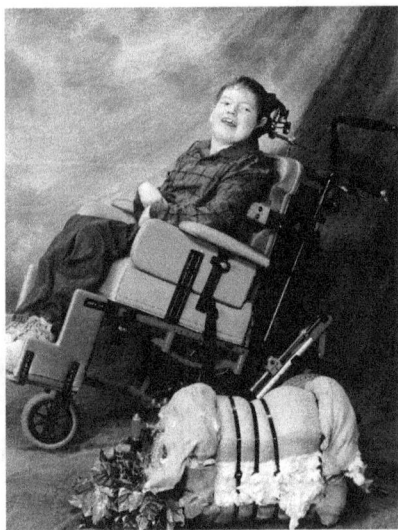

a detrimental effect on his overall health. The brain damage slowed the blood flow through his veins and arteries. His curved back and abnormal tone along with his weak upper-body strength had a detrimental effect on his health.

Another year and another holiday season passed and New Year's Day heralded in 2003. In our pile of Christmas cards and letters was one from the Nortons. A picture of Janell was enclosed. I reread the letter several times. Janet recounted in the letter the lessons God had taught their family through Janell's handicaps. Many of those lessons I could relate to well as God had taught me many of the same things. I wondered if God had a purpose for suffering in the lives of each of his children—perhaps everyone suffers to some degree. It just doesn't always look the same. Justin's and Janell's handicaps were similar, and the lessons God taught our families were similar. It made me wonder if suffering in the lives of others and the struggles to let go of self and learn to trust in a sovereign God were just as painful for others as it was for us, though circumstances may be very different. I was finding I had a compassion for the struggles of others—regardless of the trial—that I had never known before.

March came and the weather began to warm. I felt that perhaps we had passed through the cold and flu season of January and February unscathed, and I was beginning to relax when Justin once again got sick. No one else in the house was sick. At first I thought perhaps spring allergies had arrived since we had been extremely careful to avoid illness, but within forty-eight hours, Justin was struggling to breathe. It was not long before I was accompanying him in an ambulance to Lubbock, where he was admitted to a children's ICU unit, and we found ourselves in the same children's wing of the hospital we had left so many years earlier.

Although Justin had pneumonia again, I was relieved when they decided it was not necessary to intubate him. I had never considered the possibility of intubating Justin, and I realized how unprepared I was to make decisions regarding how and if we should prolong his life. After a couple of days of intensive breathing treatments, Justin began to cough and clear his lungs. While in the hospital, a second diuretic was added to our list of daily meds since he was now taking the maximum dosage of Lasix.

Once he was moved out of the ICU and into a room, his nurse suggested we give him a bed bath and clean him up a bit since he had been too sick for anyone to worry about such things. Justin was now sixteen years old. Although he was small, he no longer had the physical body of a young boy. After he was clean and once more in a clean bed with freshly washed hair, we discovered to our amusement that it was difficult to find a razor in the children's wing. As he had grown, I had simply attended to his changing needs. It had never dawned on me that others might be surprised to discover he had a red beard to match his now wavy, auburn hair.

Justin never regained adequate 02 stats to allow him to breathe room air, but within a week, we were happy to once more be leaving the hospital. Since he already had an oxygen concentrator at home, the doctor in charge of his care ordered portable oxygen bottles to be added to his list of home health needs.

A few weeks later Dr. Linton examined Justin at his follow-up visit. Afterward, the kids took Justin out into the waiting room and Dr. Linton and I talked.

"Justin has been one very sick boy," Dr. Linton said kindly, "but he looks as if he is doing much better. I was a bit concerned about his 02 stats, but he seems to be doing well on a low rate of oxygen." She looked at me with compassion and patience as she asked, "Do you have any concerns about his care or his recent illness?"

"Do you think his 02 stats will continue to improve and that he might wean off the oxygen?" I asked. I knew the answer in my heart, but I wanted to hear it.

"It's always possible." However, it's more likely he'll continue to need just a little boost to keep his 02 stats up. He's probably going to continue to be very susceptible to pneumonia." She looked at me for a few seconds before she continued, and I felt as though she were trying to read my reactions to her last statement. I knew he was becoming more medically fragile and so her statement had not surprised me. She continued, "Have you thought about whether you would want him on a ventilator should he need to be intubated?" Again she looked at me carefully before she added, "Or whether you want him to be resuscitated if something were to happen and his heart stops or he stops breathing?"

In my heart I knew God was sovereign and in control. I knew he alone was the commander of life and death, but I also knew I was responsible for the decisions I made regarding Justin's health and I was afraid what the future might hold and what might happen.

I answered her carefully. "I'm not sure how I feel about intubating him or resuscitation, but I know I don't want to make decisions at a critical time or be in a position where I'm not sure what to do, so I guess that's something I need to think about and pray about."

Dr. Linton was compassionate and kind. She suggested I take the paperwork required for Do Not Resuscitate (DNR) orders home and think about those decisions. We also talked about how difficult it was to care for Justin in the hospital—especially when we were well equipped for his care at home. If we had skilled nursing care, we might not have to hospitalize him again. Dr. Linton suggested hospice care.

It was a weighty decision and I spent much time in prayer about it. I knew I was responsible for the decisions I made; however, I had peace knowing that ultimately, whatever decision I made, God is still sovereign. I knew that while my decisions could and would impact the lives of others—especially my children—they could not save or destroy without God's consent for he alone is sovereign over life and death. Two weeks later, I returned the DNR orders to Dr. Linton's office and she contacted hospice.

Hospice was in my opinion the best program we were ever on. Instead of our going to an office somewhere to fill out paperwork or spending time mailing forms back and forth, the hospice representatives came to the house and spent a lot of time accessing Justin's needs and the needs of our family.

They picked up his medications and brought them to the house, and we had skilled nursing care once more.

One of Justin's nurses was a young mom named Tina, and all of us loved her. She was compassionate and kind, yet fun and full of life. The nurses came two to three times a week. While they were there, they helped with his care, took his vital signs, and talked to us. Hospice even provided some counseling for our family. Hospice was a difficult decision, but it was proving to be a good decision for our family.

☞ Chapter 39 ☜

Farewell

But thank God! He gives us victory over sin
and death through our Lord Jesus Christ.
1 Corinthians 15:57

May of 2003 marked the second anniversary of Robby's death. When I looked at my boys, I was amazed at how much they had grown and changed in just two short years. That summer the kids and I divided our half-acre garden into several smaller sections. The previous year we had reduced the size of the plot slightly by planting a row of cedar trees on the north side, which was just inside our north property line. This time we fenced a fifty-by-fifty-foot section and limited our garden to the confines of that fenced area. Then we leveled the rest of the plot and began to sprig Bermuda grass that we hauled from the ditch. We sat down and decided what vegetables everyone liked to eat and limited our produce selection to only what we enjoyed ourselves.

When we finished the fence, it was almost too late to

plant much, but we tilled the plot and used a hand-pushed garden plow to make a few rows for tomatoes, peppers, corn, squash, and okra. A few weeks later, we also planted watermelon and a few pumpkins to decorate our porch in the fall. Not selling at the market had allowed us to do more work in the yard, and we planted a few more trees. The boys designed a flowerbed around the risers of our septic tank to hide the area. Filled with irises and zinnias, it quickly became one of my favorite parts of the yard.

Justin remained well and the summer passed peacefully and quietly. Now thirteen and fourteen with late summer and fall birthdays just on the horizon, Jacob and Jerrod both had jobs spraying cotton and were gone several hours a day for many weeks. Nana continued to come and help in the evenings. We never replaced Stacy, and now that Justin was on hospice, he no longer qualified for the CLASS program that had brought us Stacy in the first place. The hospice nurses came several times a week and helped with his care, but I managed the bulk of his care during the day. I didn't mind—it was a labor of love. I fed Justin each morning and again at noon. Every morning I bathed him, shaved him, and dressed him for the day. I changed his bed and washed his sheets and towels. When he cried, I comforted him and when he smiled, I smiled. Although I had done all of these things for years, I now did them not because I had to . . . but because I wanted to. I enjoyed serving him. Although he never spoke a word, I found great pleasure in his company.

As fall approached, I struggled to keep fear from overwhelming me regarding Justin and winter colds. Every one of us was again inoculated against the flu. Though there was some debate as to whether it was worth the risk for Justin to do the same, Dr. Linton and I finally decided, and he got the shot. Although he did run a fever for a few days, his reaction to the shot was not bad.

The previous year, in the fall of 2002, our homeschool group had started a drama program and hired a drama coach to instruct the kids. My children had wanted to participate, but I wasn't sure we could handle the rigorous practice schedule without Stacy's help so I chose not to let them participate that year. However, after attending the spring plays, they were even more eager to join. Once again, I hesitated because of the inevitable exposure to colds but finally decided I couldn't put their lives on hold. I didn't want us to live our lives as though we were waiting for Justin's to end. I clung to the knowledge that God was in control, and it was possible our family would be blessed with Justin's presence for many more years. So as fall 2003 approached, I consented and the kids signed up for drama.

Participating in drama was a real sacrifice that year simply because I did not have a caretaker for Justin during the day. We took him with us most of the time, though sometimes I was able to leave the kids at class. My mother would pick them up when she got off work and bring them home when she came in the evening to help with Justin.

As the holiday season drew near and winter's icy grip began to take hold, our hospice counselor and Justin's nurse began talking to me about making pre-arranged funeral plans. Justin's condition had changed very little since spring, and it seemed strange to talk about making funeral arrangements, but they suggested it would be much easier to make plans while Justin was well than to make plans if Justin should take a turn for the worse. It took some time to adjust to the idea, but I realized that making funeral arrangements would not change God's sovereignty or his timing in Justin's life. So after the holidays passed, I made an appointment to meet with the funeral director to pick out a casket and make a few other arrangements. Shortly after Robby had died, I had purchased a burial plot next to him, so that was one part of the arrangements I did not have to handle. It was difficult. I was glad when it was done and I could just file the papers away and not think about it.

January passed and February was almost over, and it seemed as though my fears were unfounded—we had made it through fall and most of winter without a single illness. The last month of winter was quickly passing, and spring was just around the corner. I looked forward to the arrival of March and longer and warmer days with anticipation.

On Saturday, February 28, it began to rain. I typically loved the rain because the moisture was always needed, but rain also isolated us from the outside world, which brought mixed blessings. While muddy roads meant no guests in our home and gave us extra time to be together as a family, it also prevented any of Justin's caregivers from coming since the road we had originally planned to build and gravel to the county road had never been done; only a dirt road spanned the couple of hundred yards to the paved county road.

That evening while I was feeding Justin, I thought he seemed a little warm to the touch. By the time he went to bed, it was evident he was running a fever. I gave him Acetaminophen and put him to bed. During the night, he once again felt hot to the touch. His fever had returned, so I gave him another dose of Acetaminophen. I continued to check on him frequently throughout the night. The next morning I called Tina, his hospice nurse, and told her he was running a fever and appeared to be coming down with a cold. Tina then called Dr. Linton, picked up an antibiotic prescription for Justin, and brought it to me. Because of the rain, the roads were almost impassable, so I met her at the highway to get Justin's antibiotic.

On Monday afternoon, the roads had dried some and Tina managed to get her car to our house to check on Justin and take his vital signs. By that time both Jennifer and Jacob were also running fevers and coughing. It appeared that we had contracted something viral, but I did not know where we got the virus or when. Justin was sleepy and he didn't want to eat, but we were able to keep his fever somewhat under control with Acetaminophen. Thankfully, his feeding tube allowed me to keep him well hydrated without agitating him by trying to force liquids by mouth. That night I slept very little. I kept a close watch on Justin's fever and tried to make sure he was comfortable. I did his breathing treatments every three hours. He seemed to sleep better propped up in the recliner, so I made him comfortable in the living room until after midnight. Then when he became restless, I carried him to his room and rocked him in his waterbed until he went to sleep just before dawn.

Tuesday morning Justin appeared to be worse. He was coughing some and I had upped his breathing treatments to every two hours in an attempt to break up the congestion in his lungs. When Tina arrived that day, she listened to him and told me what I already knew—his lungs were full. Once more, he had pneumonia. She spent most of the day with us helping with Justin's breathing treatments, but even with the assistance of oxygen, his breathing was labored. That evening, Nana came at her usual time and helped with his care. Justin didn't eat much, but she managed to get him to eat a few bites. By the time she left, he was sleeping.

Later that evening, my dear friend Penny came by to check on us. I met her at the door.

"So how is your crew today?" she asked. She knew Justin and my other children were all sick. "Before I come in, do y'all need anything? Can I run to the store for you and pick up something?"

"We're good," I told her as I opened the door. "We had soup for supper and everyone is ready for bed and camping out upstairs in Jacob's room."

"How's Justin?" she asked.

"I just put him in bed. He still has a fever, but it seems to be under control and not too high. He won't eat though, and he's been sleepier today. He's still very sick."

She studied my face for a minute and I could tell she was concerned for both Justin and me. "Would you like a cup of coffee or something? I have decaf."

"That sounds good," Penny said as she followed me into the kitchen. "Would you feel better if we take our coffee into Justin's room? I'd be happy to sit with you in his room for a while." We carried our cups into Justin's room, and I pulled up another chair beside the one at Justin's bedside. His breathing was shallow, and he took long pauses between breaths. Penny sat with me by his bedside for several hours.

We didn't discuss Justin's condition; we didn't need to—we both knew. And so we just sat there together without talking much at all. She stayed until after midnight. After she left, I rested my head on the edge of Justin's waterbed and dozed for a couple of hours.

As morning began to dawn, Justin became restless and uncomfortable. I gave him some more Acetaminophen to reduce his fever, but surprisingly, when I took his temperature, it was almost normal. He refused to eat, so I just gave him his morning medication and plenty of electrolytes to help keep him hydrated. Then I gave him a warm shower, hoping it would make him feel better.

By this time, Jerrod was also sick. Jacob, Jerrod, and Jennifer spent most of the day upstairs in Jacob's room playing games, listening to audio books, and watching movies. Tina arrived midmorning with plans to stay most of the day if she was needed. We continued to give Justin breathing treatments and do our best to keep him comfortable. Late that afternoon, Justin began to relax; although his breathing was shallow, he seemed to breathe easier. However, despite the fluids we were giving him, he had remained dry all day. Tina said his kidneys may have quit functioning. I decided to call my brother, who lived in New Mexico, to see if he would come after he got off work.

Since Justin was resting and it was almost time for my mother to arrive, Tina decided to go home for a while and get some sleep. Hospice had scheduled nurses to come and stay with Justin after my mother's time ended at eight o'clock so that I could get some rest. Tina planned to come back around two in the morning. The roads had finally dried, but more rain was in the forecast, so I wasn't sure if the nurses would be able to get in and out. Although I had slept very little for two nights, I felt capable of staying up with him once more if needed.

Nana arrived at six o'clock, which was her usual time. She was pleased to see that he appeared to be breathing easier and although he was sleepy, he did not appear to be uncomfortable or irritable. He didn't eat, but Nana gave him his medicine and made sure he had plenty of fluids. Then she changed his clothes and got him ready for bed. When she left, he was sleeping quietly.

Justin's hospice nurse arrived just as Nana was leaving. Before she assessed him, Jacob, Jerrod, Jennifer, and I gathered around Justin's bed for evening prayers. I had been honest with them about the situation, and they all understood that our time with Justin was limited. After prayers, they each told Justin goodnight and told him how much they loved him before they headed to bed. Jennifer was last to leave his room. She kissed him softly on the forehead before she left and whispered in his ear, "I love you, Justin." They all went upstairs to sleep in Jacob's room. While the nurse assessed Justin, I settled them in bed.

Justin's breathing was shallow and I was thankful my brother Michael was on his way. I decided to call my other brother, J.J., as well. He didn't live far and I knew he would be there soon. When I went back to Justin's room, he was no longer sleeping soundly and his respiration rate had increased, so I sat and rocked him and sang to him softly. His nurse was concerned, and she stepped out of the room to call Tina. My brother Michael arrived and joined me in Justin's room. Penny and Tina arrived almost simultaneously. A few minutes later, I stepped out of Justin's room to speak to my brother. I was only gone a minute when his nurse called me back to Justin's side.

Justin's breathing slowed just as I reached his bedside and I lifted him in my arms as he took his last breath. I held him there for a few minutes and softly whispered, "I love you." As I gently laid him back on his bed, I ran my fingers through his hair one last time, and then Penny and Tina led me from his room.

On March 3, 2004, at ten o'clock in the evening, Justin was freed from the handicapped body that had enslaved him for almost twelve years. I stood at the window in the living room for a long time. The rain had started again, and its gentle rhythm was soothing. Though my grief was so heavy it hurt to breathe, my heart was at peace as I handed the blessing on loan to me back to the one from whom he had come.

⌐ Chapter 40 ⌐

Remembering

---

*And we know that God causes everything to work
together for the good of those who love God and are called
according to his purpose for them.*
Romans 8:28

August 7, 2011. I sit on the grass and arrange the flowers
in the vase, their bright artificial color making a pretty
display. I pull green runners of grass away from the stones
and look in awe at the date carved in granite—August 7,
1986. Have twenty-five years really passed since I gave birth
to a beautiful, redheaded little baby boy?

I think back, not to the day of his birth, but to a bright
summer day five years after it. We celebrated that day he was
five—presents for Justin and his brothers, a cake with cars
on it, crayons and school supplies for our new venture into
homeschooling, and new shoes he thought he didn't need.
Who needs shoes when the summer days are warm and the

green grass feels soft to bare feet? It was a year of abundance—abundant rain, abundant grass, abundant joy.

So much can change in a year. One year later when we brought him home for his birthday, the bright, comical, talkative little boy was forever changed. There were no pictures and no cake. Only presents we opened for him, toys we hoped he might someday hold—toys that would be put away never to be used.

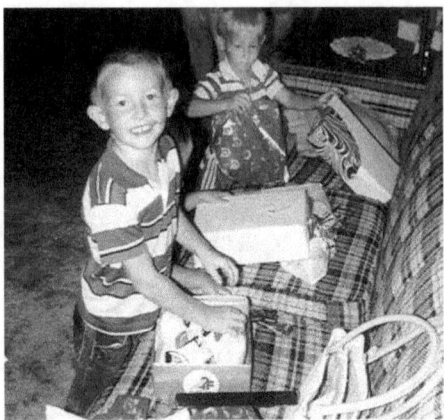

As I pull away more grass runners and uncover the gray stone, I find I am just as awed at the second date carved in the rock—March 3, 2004. Seven years have passed since he left our earthly home. I grieved that night of his death, just as I grieved that day when we brought him home for his sixth birthday . . . that deep, heart-wrenching grief that hurts the chest and steals the breath.

I grieve again, but the hurt is not so deep because I am reminded of the life that forever changed mine. His journey through this world was short—only seventeen years—but I was blessed that his journey was a major part of mine as we traveled those years together. It was a journey through deep grief, abandonment, intense anger, heartache, surrender, grace, and happiness. And in the end, there was a peace beyond understanding.

Justin's passing, both times, brought pain. But his presence—especially the child who would never walk or talk again—taught me the truth about myself and my own brokenness. His handicaps gave me a glimpse of the handicapped condition of my own heart and the unchanging nature of God.

This journey with Justin taught me that God is still good even when circumstances are not. God is still good even when I'm not. And God is still good whether I believe he is or not. God used Justin's life to teach me that joy does not depend on our circumstances, but rather it is a condition of the heart. I learned that true joy—that "dance in the kitchen" gladness—flows out of a heart that is truly grateful. And peace and contentment are found in a heart that trusts in God's sovereignty regardless of circumstances.

And so, I take flowers and remember Justin and with a heart that overflows with gratitude and joy as I remember the journey.

www.ingramcontent.com/pod-product-compliance
Lightning Source LLC
LaVergne TN
LVHW051454080426
835509LV00017B/1763